UNIVERSAL DESIGN

UNIVERSAL DESIGN

A Manual of Practical Guidance for Architects

Selwyn Goldsmith

with PRP Architects

CAD drawings by Jeanette Dezart

Architectural Press

OXFORD   AUCKLAND   BOSTON   JOHANNESBURG   MELBOURNE   NEW DELHI

Architectural Press
An imprint of Butterworth-Heinemann
Linacre House, Jordan Hill, Oxford OX2 8DP
225 Wildwood Avenue, Woburn, MA 01801-2041
A division of Reed Educational and Professional Publishing Ltd

℞ A member of the Reed Elsevier plc group

First published 2000

British Library Cataloguing in Publication Data
Goldsmith, Selwyn
   Universal design: a manual of practical guidance for
   architects
   1. Universal design 2. Architectural design 3. Architecture –
   Human factors 4. Architecture and the physically handicapped
   I. Title II. Dezart, Jeanette
   720.8'7

ISBN 0 7506 4785X

Library of Congress Cataloguing in Publication Data
A catalogue record for this book is available from the Library of Congress

Cover design by Helen Alvey of PRP Architects.
Composition by Scribe Design, Gillingham, Kent, UK
Printed and bound in Great Britain

Contents

Preface

Designing for the disabled is about making buildings accessible to and usable by people with disabilities. Universal design is about making buildings safe and convenient for all their users, including people with disabilities. A theme of this book is the similarities and differences of the two, between their correspondences and affinities on the one hand, and their discordancies and diverse methodologies on the other.

In 1961, the year after my architectural studies were completed and I had become a registered architect, I was commisioned by the Polio Reseach Fund in conjunction with the Royal Institute of British Architects to undertake a reseach project whose aim would be the production of a book to be called *Designing for the Disabled*. It was a topic I knew nothing about and one that at the time was nowhere on the agenda of practising architects – the idea that buildings ought as a matter of course to be accessible to people with disabilities was then unheard of. Professionally inexperienced though I was, the credential I had which appealed to those who appointed me was that I was myself a person with a severe physical disability, the consequence of acquiring a polio virus in 1956.

First published in 1963 by RIBA Publications, *Designing for the Disabled* became a standard textbook for practising architects. The second edition came in 1967, and the third, a bulky book of more than 500 pages, in 1976. I was subsequently disinclined to produce a fourth edition, first because it would have been a daunting chore, and second and more importantly, because I was troubled by the ethos that the book reflected, the presumption that disabled people ought to be set apart, packaged together and treated as being different from normal people.

Designing for the Disabled – The New Paradigm, my next and very different book, was published by Architectural Press in 1997. With technical data and the findings of relevant research studies interspersed, it was a mix of autobiography, history, legislation, politics and my thoughts on how the Part M building regulation, *Access and facilities for disabled people*, might be reconstituted in line with the principles of universal design. Drawing on the social model of disability, I explained that 'the disabled' of the book's title were people who could be *architecturally disabled* because buildings were impossible or very difficult for them to use, but would not be disabled or subject to discrimination had they been designed to be convenient for everyone. As well as people with disabilities, those to be found among them included pushchair users, small children and – with regard to the usage of public toilets – women in general.

It was in early 1999 when the 1976 edition of RIBA Publications' *Designing for the Disabled* had finally run out of print that I was prompted to fill the gap that the New Paradigm book had left untouched – the need that there was for an authoritative design guidance manual on universal design. The form of the book that I envisaged quickly took shape. Aimed specifically at practising architects, it would be focused principally on the design of public and employment buildings and the component features of them. It would be packed with diagrams, ones presenting design information in a form which architects could readily refer to when working on their screens or drawing boards. To keep it slim its scope would be limited to information and advice which could be conveyed by means of diagrams. And while the diagrams would be instructive they would not be prescriptive since universal design is precluded by the setting of minimum design standards, whether or not they be nationally mandated.

For the realisation of the book I set myself two conditions. One was that the book's diagrams should desirably be drawn by Louis Dezart. The other, linked to my intention that the diagrams should wherever feasible demonstrate actual examples of built practice rather than theorised notions, was that professional colleagues in an architectural practice would work with me on its preparation.

In the years from 1969 to 1972 I had been the buildings editor of the *Architects' Journal.* Louis Dezart was then the *AJ*'s drawings editor, and in 1973 when I asked him to suggest who might prepare the diagrams for the third edition of *Designing for the Disabled,* he offered to do them himself. And as anyone who has glanced at the book may know, the hundreds of splendid drawings that came with it were of a quality unrivalled in any comparable publication.

On his retirement in 1993 Louis moved with his family to France, the link being that his grandfather was French. Over the years we kept in touch, and I contacted him in April 1999 when the idea of a book on universal design took shape. No, was the message on the phone, he was content in retirement, and reverting back to producing diagrams for books was not at all what he wanted to do. But his daughter Jeanette (whom I had last met when she was six years old) was a skilled CAD technician, and she might be interested. And in any event the family would be delighted if my wife Becky and I were to visit them.

With a synopsis for the book but no publisher in view, we travelled in late June 1999 to the west of France, to the small village of Anchais in the Vendée. Jeanette was not merely interested, she was positively enthusi-

astic. French Motorways was her employer, and from an office south of Paris the contract work she was doing with an engineering team was seasonal. Come November she would have a four-month break, and what she would most like to be doing during the months at home was tackling the challenging task of generating the book's CAD diagrams. The prospect also appealed to Louis – he would be ready to help where sketches were needed.

Peter Randall, a retired director of PRP Architects, was a friend of many years. In April 1999 he and his wife Rosemary invited us to meet for lunch at a restaurant in Hampton, where among other matters we talked about my proposed book and my plan to have an architectural practice work with me on it. I subsequently discussed the idea with Peter Phippen, the chairman of PRP Architects; he was already pressing the concept of universal design in his office and was attracted by the prospect of cooperating with me on the project. The proviso was that a publisher had first to be found, with the terms of the contract for the production of the book being suitable for all concerned.

In August 1999 I wrote to Architectural Press. In response, yes, they said, they liked the idea of a book on universal design and felt it could usefully complement their *Metric Handbook.* Were it to go ahead, their trust was that it could, like *Metric Handbook,* become a book that would be regularly revised and updated. A draft contract came to me in September and from then on Jeanette Dezart, PRP Architects and I were able to push ahead with the book's preparation.

Starting in November 1999, Jeanette's first task was to establish in association with Architectural Press exactly how the CAD diagrams were to be formatted so that they were suitable for publication – the tests made were with drafts of the complex anthropometric diagrams that appear on pages 28 and 29. As work on the book progressed there was a steady increase in the number of diagrams required for it; from an initial estimate of 230 the final figure was close to 370. An additional task that Jeanette took on board was to prepare layouts of all the diagram pages in the form they would be when the book was printed; this was an exacting operation which involved deciding which diagrams would go where, the scale to which they would be reproduced, and how the headings, captions, dimension lines and annotations would be fitted in on each page. And along the way her job was made more tiresome by the changes frequently made to the drawings and the composition of the diagram pages.

Jeanette persevered. Continuously cheerful, forebearing and good-humoured, she was determined from the start that the entire operation would be completed in accord with the rigorous professional standards she set herself. She remained unperturbed when it became apparent that the four months allocated to the project would not be sufficient. In March 2000 she returned to her French Motorways work, now as clerk of works on the earthworks of a motorway bridge over the Seine near Paris. Regularly on a Friday evening she travelled 250 miles home, spent much of the weekend on diagram work, and returned to Paris late on the Sunday evening or early Monday morning.

The practical help, support and encouragement that Becky gave me through the many months I spent working on the book not only made the whole endeavour manageable but also more rewarding and enjoyable. On the June 1999 trip to Anchais she did most of the car driving, found disabled-accessible hotels for us, and was delighted by the friendships she formed with the Dezart family. The trip was repeated in late June 2000 when Jeanette, Louis and I occupied ourselves over three days checking final drafts of the book's diagrams while Becky spent pleasing hours with Maureen, Sean and Tina.

Rewarding friendships both for Becky and myself came also from the association with PRP Architects. On the production of the book the arrangement which Peter Phippen made with Maurice Heather, an associate in the practice, was that two of their architects,

Anne-Marie Nicholson and Lesley Gibbs, would assist me, and this they did splendidly. On how the concept of universal design should be communicated by way of the book's diagrams, we realised how informative it was to draw on relevant examples of built practice. The high repute in which PRP Architects is held is linked principally to its housing expertise, in particular to the extensive range of social housing schemes it has worked on with housing associations over many years. The house plans in the book all come from schemes designed by PRP Architects, as do examples of bathroom and wc layouts and a number of other housing features. The cover of the book was designed in conjunction with Architectural Press by Helen Alvey, a PRP graphic designer.

The link with RHWL Architects was arranged by Peter Phippen, and from it came the diagrams illustrating built examples of hotel guestrooms and tiered seating in cinemas and theatres. The valuable cooperation we had, both on providing the examples for illustration in the book and advising on their presentation, was with Colin Hobart on the hotel guestrooms and Barry Pritchard and Suzie Bridges on the tiered seating and wheelchair seating spaces.

As noted earlier, the scope of the book is limited to items for which information can be conveyed by way of diagrams, meaning that issues such as hearing-aid systems, acoustics, heating, ventilation and floor finishes are not examined. At the same time, the book's coverage could advantageously have been extended: it became evident as it was being drafted that the scope for explaining and illustrating the concept of universal design in the field of architecture and buildings was unlimited. Had time and resources been available, many more illustrative diagrams could have been put into the book, and a much broader range of types of public buildings and housing could have been covered. But closure lines had to be drawn. One determinant was the delivery date specified in the contract. Another was the timetable that Jeanette Dezart had set herself; both for her and for myself that imposed a firm discipline, one without which the venture might well have faltered.

Such errors and misapprehensions as may be found in this book are my responsibility. Simple mistakes could be rectified should the book be reprinted, but more ample revisions would need to wait for a second edition should cause for that occur. In this connection the arrangement I made with Peter Phippen when PRP Architects agreed to cooperate with me on the first edition was confirmed in the terms of my contract with Architectural Press. It was that if a second edition of *Universal Design* were needed it would not be my responsibility – the book would be revised and updated by PRP Architects, and they would inherit the copyright in it.

Should there be a second edition of this book the format, coverage and content of it will be for PRP Architects to determine. To tackle the task they would welcome feedback from practising architects and others on how they judge this book and the ideas they have on how in a second edition it might be improved. Correspondence should be addessed to PRP Architects, 82 Bridge Road, Hampton Court, East Molesey, Surrey, KT8 9HF.

Acknowledgements

As has been made clear in the preface, the principal debt of gratitude that I owe for the realisation of this book is to Jeanette Dezart – had it not been for her I doubt it would ever have come to fruition. In preparing her CAD diagrams she was helpfully advised by Architectural Press colleagues – on behalf of her and myself thanks are expressed to the production controller Pauline Sones, the electronics editor Alex Hollingsworth and the book's typesetter, John Gardiner of Scribe Design. Relatedly, my thanks go to Neil Warnock-Smith, Architectural Press's technical publishing director, and the desk editor Sue Hamilton.

Again for reasons made clear in the preface, my other major indebtedness is to Peter Phippen and PRP Architects. Diagrams in the book illustrating building work designed by PRP Architects are 5.39, 7.42–5, 7.70, 7.72, 7.78–9 and 9.1–11.

Diagrams illustrating work undertaken by RHWL Architects are 8.4 and 8.6–8. Advice relating to the Arc cinema at Stockton-on-Tees was given by the Arc management and Burdus Access Management.

Diagrams illustrating the turning spaces of electric scooters (5.22 and 5.23) were informed by on-site surveys made in cooperation with the staff of the Kingston-on-Thames Shopmobility service.

Company catalogues and associated technical information from which diagrams have been derived are Days Medical (2.2, 2.4 and 2.5); Nicholls and Clarke (2.9, 7.10, 7.19a, 7.65 and 7.66); Ashdale Healthcare (2.6 and 2.7); Dorma (5.17); Sealmaster (5.39); Wessex Medical Company (6.24 and 6.28); Sesame Access Systems (6.25); Access Solutions (6.26 and 6.27); Stannah Lifts (6.29); Neaco (7.80 and 7.81).

For advice on anthropometric matters I am grateful to Bob Feeney of RFA Consultants. For matters associated with the administration of building regulations I am indebted to Andrew Burke of the building regulations division of the Department of the Environment, Transport and the Regions and Andrew Lang of the building control office of the Development Department of the Scottish Executive.

1 Universal design, buildings and architects

The bottom-up route to universal design

Broadly, universal design means that the products which designers design are universally accommodating, that they cater conveniently for all their users. On the route towards this goal a product that was initially designed primarily for the mass market of normal able-bodied people could have been subsequently been refined and modified – the effect, with accommodation parameters being extended, being that it would suit all its other potential users as well, including people with disabilities.

Five examples of this universal design process are cited, none of the products concerned being ones that in previous forms had been geared to suit people with disabilities. First, the remote-control television operator. Second, the personal computer – as word processor, electronic-mail communicator and, through the Internet, information provider. Third, the mobile telephone. Fourth, the microwave cooker. Fifth, the standard car with off-the-peg features such as automatic drive, central door-locking, electronic windows and power-assisted steering. Good design for everyone, it may be noted, is good for disabled people.

The methodology of this design process is termed bottom up. The comparison is with a product initially designed to meet the special needs of a particular group of people with disabilities, one that was subsequently modified so that it suited normal able-bodied people as well; here the design process would have been top down.

In the case of the five bottom-up examples cited, the extension of accommodation parameters to take in people with disabilities was achieved by virtue of modern technology, most importantly electronic technology. There is not therefore a straight analogy here with the architect, who when designing a building aims to make it universally accommodating and convenient for all of its potential users, since electronic technology cannot facilitate the accomplishment of all the activities undertaken by each and every person who uses a building. But it does, for instance, serve well where automatic-opening doors are installed as normal provision to make it easier for everyone to get into and around public buildings.

The architect who takes the bottom-up route to universal design works on the premise that the building users he or she is serving, including those with disabilities, are all people who can be treated as normal people. The architect does not start with the presumption that people with disabilities are abnormal, are peculiar and different, and that, in order to make buildings accessible to them, they should be packaged together and then, with a set of special-for-the-disabled accessibility standards, have their requirements presented in top-down mode as add-ons to unspecified normal provision.

With regard to public buildings, ones that are used by all kinds of people, the route to universal design is illustrated by diagram **1.1** with its pyramid of building users. For a building that is to cater conveniently for the needs of all its potential users, the architect, moving up from one row to the next, looks to expand the accommodation parameters of normal provision, and by doing so minimise the need for special provision to be made for people with disabilities. The aim will be to ensure, so far as possible, that no one will be threatened by architectural disability – from being unable or finding it very difficult to use a building or a feature of it on account of the way it was designed – or (meaning in effect the same thing) be subjected to architectural discrimination.

Against these criteria, judgements are made on how architects have tended to perform over the last fifty years or so, the subjects under review being public buildings such as theatres, department stores, pubs, hotels and restaurants – ones which among their other amenities have public toilets for the benefit of their customers.

In row 1 at the foot of the eight-level pyramid are fit and agile people, those who can run and jump, leap up stairs, climb perpendicular ladders, dance exuberantly and carry loads of heavy baggage. In row 2 are the generality of normal adult able-bodied people, those who, while not being athletic, can walk wherever needs or wishes may take them, with flights of stairs not troubling them. Scoring as at pointer A, architects do as a rule cater well enough for these people. It needs, however, to be noted that there are no small children in rows 1 and 2.

Like those in rows 1 and 2, the people in row 3 are in the main also normal able-bodied people, and in the public realm the architect frequently fails them. These are women, the users of public buildings who when they attempt to use public toilets are regularly subjected to architectural discrimination because the number of wcs provided for them is typically less than half the number of urinals and wcs that men are given, the effect being that they can be obliged to join a long queue or abandon the quest.

In row 4 are elderly people who, although perhaps going around with a walking stick, do not regard themselves as being 'disabled'. Along with them are people with infants in pushchairs, who – men as well as women – can be architecturally disabled when looking to use public toilets on account of stairs on the approach to them and the lack of space in wc compartments for both the adult and the infant in the pushchair.

In row 5 are ambulant people who have disabilities. Broadly, the building users who are in rows 3, 4 and 5 are people who would not be architecturally disabled if normal provision in buildings were suitable for them, if it were standard practice for architects to design buildings to the precepts of universal design, with public toilet facilities being more accommodating and conveniently reachable, and steps and stairs being comfortably graded and equipped with handrails to both sides. Across Britain, however, that is not by any means a general rule, the effect being as shown in pointer B where the squiggle in rows 3, 4 and 5 indicates building users who could when new buildings are designed be conveniently accommodated by suitable normal provision, but often are not.

The people in row 6 are independent wheelchair users, and with them Part M comes into the reckoning. In the years since 1985 new public buildings in Britain have had to be designed in compliance with the Part M building regulation, meaning that access provision for disabled people has to be made in and around them. The Part M process operates top-down, and it focuses on making special provision in buildings. It is independent wheelchair users who govern its 'for the disabled' prescriptions, and an effect of this when the design guidance in the Part M Approved Document is followed is that the needs of independent wheelchair users may be satisfied, but not necessarily those of ambulant disabled people or people in wheelchairs who when using public buildings need to be helped by someone else. The outcome of this selective top-down procedure is shown in pointer C, with the squiggle denoting the people in rows 5, 4 and 3 whose needs may not be entirely taken care of when they use public buildings.

universal design + special provisions.

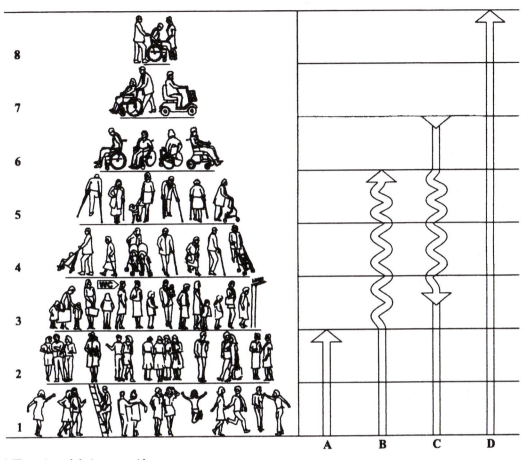

1.1 *The universal design pyramid*

The physically disabled people whose particular needs are not fully covered by Part M are at the top of the pyramid. In row 7 are wheelchair users who need another person to help them when they use public buildings, and those disabled people who drive electric scooters. In row 8, having regard in particular to the usage of public toilets, are wheelchair users who need two people to help them when they go out.

A need that people in row 8 and many of those in row 7 could have when using public buildings would be for a suitably planned unisex toilet facility where a wife could help her husband, or a husband his wife. This would be special rather than normal provision, but for universal design purposes it would be

admissible; the rule is that where normal provision cannot cater for everyone, supplementary special provision may be made.

Of the people with disabilities shown in the pyramid, one – in row 5 – is a blind person led by a guidedog. The others, either ambulant disabled or wheelchair users, are all people with locomotor impairments. It is these who when using public buildings are most vulnerable to architectural discrimination, for example on account of steps and stairs, confined circulation spaces, and fixtures, fittings and controls that are too high or too low to reach. And for the architect who is looking to counter architectural discrimination when designing a building on the drawing board or computer screen, it is people with locomotor impairments who can most readily benefit. By way of information conveyed on architectural drawings the scope available to help people with sensory or cognitive disabilities is tiny by comparison.

Ideally, the outcome of applying the principles of universal design would be as shown by the D pointer, indicating buildings that are entirely convenient for all their users. As has already been noted, however, the pyramid does not show children, and for them an important consideration is the height of fixtures and fittings.

The issue is exemplified by wash basins. In cloakrooms in public buildings where there is a single basin, and also where two or more basins are at the same level, it is customary for the bowl rim to be at about 820 mm above floor level. As diagram **4.11f** on page 37 shows, this is not convenient for young children. Nor, as diagrams **4.11a** and **b** show, is it convenient for standing adult people, for whom 950 mm is more suitable. There is no single level at which a wash basin can be fixed so that it suits all users.

The principles of universal design are not compromised by it not being possible to fix a wash basin at a height which will be convenient for all its users. By expanding the accommodation parameters of normal provision, with supplementary special provision being added on where appropriate, the architect's objective is to make buildings as convenient as can be for all their potential users. The operative condition is 'as convenient as can be'. There are times, as with washing at a basin, when architectural discrimination is unavoidable.

The Part M building regulation

Britain's national building regulations are functional – they ask for something such as ventilation, means of escape in the event of fire, drainage, sanitary conveniences and washing facilities to be provided at an adequate or reasonable level. In England and Wales the function that is covered by the Part M regulation is access and facilities for disabled people (in Scotland Part T, the access-for-the-disabled building standard which was the equivalent of Part M, has been assimilated into other parts of the Scottish building regulations). The design standards prescribed in the 1999 Part M Approved Document are shown in many diagrams in this book, and are the yardstick against which universal design options are measured.

For access provision in newly designed public buildings, a narrow interpretation of Part M requirements can for three reasons hinder the realisation of universal design. First, because exclusive attention to the needs of disabled people ignores many other building users who are prone to architectural discrimination, for example women in respect of public toilet facilities. Second, because of the top-down form of Part M: it comes with minimum design standards that present cut-off points, meaning that disabled people who are not accommodated by the minimum standards are liable to be excluded. Third, because of the conflicting methodologies of designing for the disabled versus designing for everyone.

The story of how the Part M regulation came to be introduced is told in *Designing for the Disabled – The New Paradigm*. It began in the 1950s when Tim Nugent was director of rehabilitation education on the Champaign Urbana campus of the University of Illinois. Many of his students were young paraplegics in wheelchairs, and the task that he set himself was to train them to manage independently, to get around on their own and undertake all the activities of daily living without assistance. Architectural barriers, he recognised, were the obstacle that stood in the way of their being able to realise their full potential for achievement and compete successfully with others for the material rewards that America offered. To set about removing the barriers he drew up the world's first-ever set of design standards for accessibility and then went on to demonstrate how the university and public buildings in Champaign and Urbana could be altered so that they were accessible to wheelchair users. He became America's national expert on the subject, and an outcome of his pioneering work was that he was asked to prepare the draft of what was to be the seminal document in access-for-the-disabled history, the initial American Standard, the 1961 A117.1 *American Standard Specifications for Making Buildings and Facilities Accessible to, and Usable by, the Physically Handicapped.*

In America, and then in Britain and elsewhere around the world, the 1961 A117.1 set the mould for access standards. It drew on four propositions, which were flawed, but which in the context of the administration of regulatory controls for accessibility have effectively remained undisturbed.

They were first, that architectural barriers in and around buildings are a threat to disabled people, but not to able-bodied people; second, that all disabled people – all those with a physical, sensory or cognitive impairment – can be disadvantaged by architectural barriers and can be emancipated where they are removed; third, that what for accessibility purposes suits wheelchair users will generally serve for all other disabled people, allowing there to be a single package of access prescriptions with a common set of design specifications; and fourth, that design specifications for disabled people can be precise and definitive – that there are 'right' solutions.

Following a meeting which Tim Nugent addressed at the Royal Institute of British Architects in October 1962, Britain took up the challenge, and the first British access standard, CP96, *Access for the disabled to buildings*, was issued by the British Standards Institution in 1967. In one significant respect, toilet facilities for disabled people, its design standards differed from those of A117.1. The American line, in accord with Nugent's determination that wheelchair users ought to be treated as though they were normal people, was that each normal toilet room for men and women in a public building should incorporate a wheelchair facility, a small-size one which was geared to suit capable wheelchair users who could manage independently but not those who needed to be helped – they could

be ignored. In Britain research findings had highlighted the lack of public toilets for severely handicapped wheelchair users who needed to be helped by their partner[1], and the need was for a design standard for a unisex facility, one that would be set apart from normal toilet provision. A key item in the 1967 CP96, this was an amenity which had never previously been tested in practice, and as feedback from users soon confirmed, the dimensions set for it – 1370 × 1750 mm – were not generous. When CP96 was revised and became BS 5810 in 1979, the design standard for a unisex toilet came with a 1500 × 2000 mm plan layout.

The Part M building regulation followed in 1987, with the guidance in its Approved Document being drawn directly from the BS 5810 access standard, including the advice for a unisex toilet; as is discussed on page 71, this facility is by no means ideal for its purpose. But through the 1990s the 1979 BS 5810 remained in place, and the design standards presented in it, including those for the unisex toilet, were virtually unchanged in the 1992 and 1999 editions of the Part M Approved Document.

With universal design the aim is that buildings should be convenient for all their users, with architectural discrimination being avoided. But as has been noted with regard to the height of wash basins (an item not covered in the Part M Approved Document), there are occasions where discrimination is unavoidable. And adherence to Part M design standards can serve to exacerbate discrimination, the operative factor being that they are geared to meeting the needs of independent wheelchair users. An example comes with lift controls, for which the Part M advice is that they are not less than 900 mm and not more than 1200 mm above floor level. As the diagrams on page 38 show, this is not convenient for standing adult people, particularly those with sight impairments.

With regard to circulation spaces in and around buildings, architectural discrimination may also be caused by adherence to the minimum standards advised for Part M purposes. The Part M rule is that passageways should have an unobstructed width of 1200 mm and internal doors a clear opening width of 750 mm; this is satisfied by 900 mm standard doorsets which give an opening width of 775 mm. The diagrams on page 47 show that this suits single-pushchair users as well as independent wheelchair users, but discriminates against wheelchair users who are pushed by a companion, electric scooter users and double-pushchair users.

A Part M requirement is that a new public building should have at least one BS 5810-type unisex toilet. In America the rule is that a wc compartment suitable for independent wheelchair users should be a feature of all toilet rooms in public buildings – it is normal provision. In Britain the BS 5810-type unisex toilet is special for disabled people – the one provided in each public building being separated from the normal provision for males and females. And for normal public toilet facilities there are no statutory rules – no minimum standards for the size of wc compartments and no conditions aimed at preventing discrimination against women.

Typical wc compartments in public toilets are not convenient for their users. Particularly for women, they are too small to manage comfortably. And on hygiene grounds they fail, there not as a rule being a wash basin within them.

The issue of public toilets and discrimination against women is discussed on page 67. In public toilets in Britain today it is common for the number of amenities that men are given (urinals and wcs) to be about twice as many as the wcs that women get, whereas for parity women ought as a rule to have twice as many toilet amenities as men.

A survey made in 1992 of toilet facilities in public buildings in London is reported in the *New Paradigm* book[2]. Four examples from it are cited. At the National Theatre there were 83 urinals and wcs for men compared with 36 wcs for women: at the Royal Festival Hall the corresponding figures were 64 and 28, at the British Museum 41 and 19, and at Liverpool Street station 49 and 20.

Alterations to existing buildings

The requirements of the Part M building regulation apply to all public buildings that are newly erected, and also to those which have been substantially demolished to leave only external walls. They do not at present (September 2000) apply to alterations to existing buildings, a relevant factor being that new buildings can be subjected to common design standards in order to achieve comprehensive accessibility, whereas the same cannot be done when existing buildings are altered.

The essential principle of universal design, the expansion of the accommodation parameters of normal provision, is, however, equally as applicable to building alterations as it is to new construction. In any existing building the provision that is there at the start is 'normal', and where alterations are made to improve the accessibility of the building, the outcome will be to extend its accommodation parameters, for example by making it accessible to wheelchair users where previously it was not. More frequently for alterations than for new buildings it may be appropriate to incorporate supplementary special provision, for example the installation of a platform lift to carry wheelchair users where there are steps on circulation routes. On the other hand, accessibility for independent wheelchair users will be precluded where entrance steps cannot be substituted or bypassed.

When any particular building is to be altered, the options there might be to enhance its accessibility and convenience for its users will be affected by a range of considerations, most importantly the costs of the operation. But even where expenditure is minimal, as for example it would be for fixing handrails to steps or stairs that had been without them, the benefits could be considerable. Correspondingly, it costs little to turn the door to a wc compartment around so that the space within is more convenient for its users, or to remove an unwanted inner door to an awkwardly tight lobby. Relatedly, fixing releasable catches for holding doors open in the passageways of public and employment buildings will be beneficial. And at the entrances to buildings of all kinds, the installation of automatic-opening doors in place of heavily-sprung self-closing doors will be welcomed by all users, not only those with disabilities.

Alterations to the public toilets in an existing building may afford the opportunity to remedy discrimination against women. In certain buildings it might be practicable to merge male and female zones so that there are unisex wc compartments, ones which with wash basins and additional space would be more convenient for their users than their predecessors.

In existing buildings where it is not feasible to replan toilet facilities and provide a separate unisex facility for disabled people, there could perhaps be the possibility of rearranging existing wc compartments so that some with wash basins in them would be wheelchair-accessible – plan examples are shown on page 80. In office buildings this practice could be convenient for staff who are wheelchair users.

In any existing public building of two or more storeys without a lift, alterations to install one, however small, would be beneficial. But desirably the lift would accommodate a wheelchair user; where structural plan constraints preclude the provision of a lift to Part M minimum design standards, a smaller lift such as that shown in diagram **6.18** would serve.

The obstacle to wheelchair access commonly presented by many existing public buildings such as high street shops and small office buildings is steps at the entrance door. While buildings of this kind are not currently subject to Part M requirements when alterations are made to them, they are subject to an important condition that applies to all buildings to which material alterations are made. It is known as the 'not worse' condition, and the relevant regulatory requirement is that the alterations made to a building should not result in provision that is less satisfactory in respect of access for disabled people than it was before.

The practical interpretation of this requirement can pose problems. Disabled people are diverse, and on account of their varying needs what may suit one could be unsuitable for another. Where steps are to be removed in order to provide wheelchair accessibility, the conflict can be between wheelchair users who need ramps and ambulant disabled people who favour steps. Even if a ramp is too steep for a person in a wheelchair to manage independently, any wheelchair user would still prefer it to no ramp at all if there is someone to push them up and help them down. Ambulant disabled people may find it very difficult or uncomfortable to cope with steep ramps and – more for going down than going up – would ask for suitable steps.

The problem does not occur in the case of new buildings designed to comply with Part M. A 1:15 ramp is manageable for wheelchair users who are being pushed and most of those who move about independently, and at the same time is not so steep as to be inconvenient for ambulant disabled people. A 1:12 ramp is less satisfactory, though not markedly so when its length is less than about 3 m. It is ramps steeper than 1:12 which can be awkward for ambulant disabled people; where they are put in place for the benefit of wheelchair users, adjoining steps ought also to be available.

Across Britain in recent years many shopkeepers and the managers of small offices have been considering what they might do to make their premises accessible to wheelchair users. Six examples in and around London are shown in the diagrams on page 62, ones that were drawn from photographs of the buildings concerned. All are of alterations which provide access for wheelchair users by way of ramps that are steeper than 1:12. But when the design proposals for them were submitted for building control approval there were none, it may be supposed, that warranted consideration on account of the not-worse condition – in each case the understanding would have been that access for the disabled was being improved.

On page 56 each of these six cases is examined, with a subjective judgement of whether the outcome was worse or not worse. For three cases, one of them with a ramp graded at 1:6, the reckoning is that it was not worse, for one that it was perhaps worse, and for two that it was worse.

The adjustments-to-buildings provisions are in Part III of the Disability Discrimination Act, the part concerned with discrimination in the area of goods, facilities, services and premises, and the Government plans for them to be brought fully into force on 1 October 2004. Under section 21 in Part III, a service provider (who may or may not be the building owner) will have two related duties in order to deliver access rights. One will be to provide auxiliary aids or services that will help disabled people make use of his services, and for these the legislative requirements became fully operable in October 1999. The other will be to do all that is reasonably possible in all the circumstances of the case to make the premises accessible to, and usable by, disabled people.

Under other provisions in Part III of the Act, a disabled person who comes across a building and finds it not as conveniently accessible to them as they reckon it could be (meaning, as they see it, that not all that could reasonably have been done has been done) will have the right to ask for the premises to be altered to take account of their particular access needs. Should the service provider reject their demands on the grounds that they are impracticable or unreasonable, and should negotiation and conciliation processes fail, the disabled person, if still dissatisfied, may sue the provider, take him or her to court and seek redress.

In May 2000 the Department for Education and Employment and the Disability Rights Commission issued a pack of consultation papers on proposals for implementing the adjustments-to-buildings provisions. These related to proposals for a new code of practice for the access rights of disabled people in Part III, proposals for regulations, and the draft of a design guide, *Overcoming physical barriers to access for disabled customers – a practical guide for smaller service providers.* A questionnaire came with the consultation pack, asking, among other matters, for suggestions on how the design guide might be improved. Affected by the responses the May 2000 draft could be substantially revised, and comment is not made here on the advice contained in it.

As has been noted, Part M design standards were governed by the concerns of independent wheelchair users, and in the access business as in other disability arenas, disabled people are commonly perceived as meaning wheelchair users. The effect is that paramountcy is afforded to independent wheelchair users, with ambulant disabled people, however many times more numerous they may be, being relegated.

In assessing the diagrams on page 62 against the not-worse condition, a factor borne in mind, however, was that steps without a ramp can be an absolute impediment for wheelchair users, whereas for ambulant disabled people a ramp without steps will as a rule not be. There is here a proviso with regard to wheelchair users; it is that a single relatively low step aligned with the door, as in **6.16a** on page 62, is not usually an absolute impediment, since an able-bodied helper can push the person in the wheelchair over it by pressing a foot on the chair's tipping lever and then shoving.

The diagrams on page 62 showing alterations to existing buildings demonstrate how difficult it may be for a service provider to determine what it might be reasonable to do to improve the accessibility of the premises to disabled people. The provider would be helped if able to refer to official guidance stating what minimum design standards would be appropriate. But given the terms of the legislative requirements, the variability of existing public buildings, the scope there might be for altering them, and a range of other considerations that makes each case unique, the application across the board of prescriptive design standards is not a viable proposition.

The three alteration schemes shown on page 62 that are judged to provide access for disabled people that is not worse than it was before are considered in the context of setting design standards for the gradient of ramps when buildings are altered. Diagram **6.17** is informative. Here is a building where it was practicable to install a ramp alongside the steps, but where the confines of the site dictated a ramp that would have a 1:6 gradient. Questions are posed by it. Given that this has access provision that affords wheelchair access and the outcome in terms of access for disabled people is not worse than it was before, ought it to be outlawed under the terms of the Disability Discrimination Act because for independent wheelchair users a 1:6 gradient is not as convenient as the 1:12 prescribed for new buildings? One way or the other in cases such as this, a law that has been introduced to prohibit discrimination against disabled people will result in discrimination.

For determining what would be reasonable in each problematical case a sensible means might be to extend the Part M building regulation to cover alterations to existing buildings. In this connection the Department for the Environment, Transport and Regions is currently (September 2000) administering a study of how the public buildings component of Part M might be improved, with views being sought on the scope there could be for extending Part M requirements to apply to existing buildings.

Discussion follows subsequently on how in practice the implementation of universal design principles might for public buildings be achieved in conjunction with satisfying the requirements of the Part M regulation. To inform the issue relevant data on the usage of public buildings is now considered.

Populations of building users

In 1990 the Department of the Environment commissioned a research project on sanitary provision for people with special needs. The purpose was to produce estimates of the proportion of building users who had special needs when using public toilets, and relatedly to present advice on provision requirements, both in respect of individual public building types and public buildings generally. The methodology was in two parts, population counts made in shopping centres around England, and interview surveys of samples of groups of building users in four towns, Carlisle, Eastbourne, Hereford and Peterborough. The premise, sustained when relevant checks were made, was that shopping centre users could be held to represent the users of public buildings generally. Selected findings are listed in Tables 1.1–1.3; a fuller record of them is in the *Designing for the Disabled – The New Paradigm*. Affected by the on-location interviews being with people of age 16 or over, these relate to adult people only.

The figures in Table 1.1 for the estimated proportion of pushchair users, wheelchair users and blind people among shopping centre users were drawn from the data obtained in the course of population counts. The figure for ambulant disabled people was derived from the way that interview questions were set. The question put to all who were interviewed was in the form 'if you are trying to use a public toilet, how important is it for you have level access, so that you don't need to use steps or stairs to get there?' Those who replied 'essential' or 'important' and said it was because of disability or a health problem were classified as 'disabled'. Of the 11.5 per cent of all shopping centre users who were classified as ambulant disabled people, 4.2 per cent were stick or crutch users and 95.8 per cent were not.

Table 1.1 Shopping centre users in an English town on a typical day

	%
Able-bodied people	84.8
Ambulant disabled people	11.5
Pushchair users	3.5
Wheelchair users	0.2
Blind people	0.02

Table 1.2 Walking ability of people in wheelchairs who are users of shopping centres

	%
Can walk without needing any support	9
Can walk with a stick/frame/crutches	47
Can walk with something to hold on to such as a rail on the side wall	18
Cannot walk at all	27

The estimate (Table 1.1) was that one person in 500 of all shopping centre users was a wheelchair user. There were 174 people in the wheelchair user sample, but there was no sensible means of establishing by way of interview questions which of them could be categorised as an independent wheelchair user. The informative question was the one that asked about walking ability, to which the responses were as listed in Table 1.2. While the finding was that some 70 per cent had some ability to walk, no reliable estimate can be made from this or associated data as to how many wheelchair users are chairbound, are able to travel independently, can get around urban streets independently and can use public buildings independently – a crude estimate drawn from relevant project findings is that it could be about 5 per cent of all wheelchair users who visit shopping centres.

Some 20 of the diagrams in this book illustrate wheelchair users who are performing one function or another independently. They are depictions of people in wheelchairs who do not have upper limb impairments; related notes on this are in the commentary to the anthropometric diagrams on page 25.

Of the pushchair users in the population of shopping centre users, some 4 per cent were users of double pushchairs. Blind people, representing one in 5000 of the population, were those seen with a guidedog or using a white stick or cane as a mobility aid.

Although shopping centre users can be equated with the users of public buildings, the proportions vary for public buildings generally, different public building types and different building user groups. With regard to disabled people, (wheelchair users and ambulant disabled people), project findings indicated that an estimated 11.7 per cent of the total population of shopping centre users on a typical day were people with locomotor impairments (Table 1.1). Against this, the proportion who were users of cinemas and theatres was 5.0 per cent, of pubs 6.6 per cent, of motorway service stations 6.9 per cent, and of railway stations 7.3 per cent. At the other end of the scale 19.8 per cent of those who used doctors' surgeries were disabled people.

Excluding doctors' surgeries, interviewees were asked about their usage of 12 public building types – department stores/supermarkets, cafes/restaurants, pubs, hotels, cinemas/theatres, museums/art galleries, swimming pools/leisure centres, sports stadia, railway stations, airport terminals, motorway service stations, and other petrol stations. When relevant data for these were analysed, the usage of an 'average' public building could be calculated, with findings as shown in Table 1.3. It indicates that whereas the proportion of shopping centre users who were disabled people was an estimated 11.7 per cent, that of the users of an average public building was 7.5 per cent.

The population of disabled people who are shopping centre users has a very different profile from that of the overall national population of people with disabilities. Comparisons with the 1988 report of the national survey of disabled people undertaken by the Office of Population Censuses and Surveys suggested that a substantial proportion of disabled people did not use any public buildings during the course of a year, particu-

Table 1.3 Estimated distribution of the population of public building users expressed as an average of the users of a range of public building types

	%
Able-bodied people	90.7
Ambulant disabled people	7.4
Pushchair users	1.9
Wheelchair users	0.1

larly those with multiple disabilities or who were elderly. The only type of building which all disabled people use is housing, either private dwelling units or communal establishments such as nursing homes or residential homes for old people.

As part of the sanitary provision research project a survey was also made of wheelchair users in nine local districts in England who were in paid employment and had a need for wheelchair-accessible toilet facilities at their place of work. Translated into national figures, the estimates were that for every 100 000 people employed in office-type buildings there were 18 wheelchair users, and for other workplaces five wheelchair users. Fuller findings are reported in the *New Paradigm* book[3].

The path to universal design: public buildings

The implementation of the precepts of universal design in respect of new public and employment buildings in Britain would ideally be mandated by a statutory instrument, for example a new building regulation which would prescribe conditions for designing buildings that would be convenient for all their users. But that is not a practicable proposition, since a building regulation necessarily operates top down, and for compliance with its requirements has prescriptions in the form of minimum design standards, ones that involve cut-off points. For universal design with its axiom of extending the accommodation parameters of normal provision, cut-off points that draw a line between inclusion and exclusion are not acceptable, and minimum design standards or generally applicable prescriptions are therefore ruled out.

For making buildings accessible to disabled people the Part M building regulation drew on an American model, Tim Nugent's 1961 American standard. For its minimum design standards the cut-off points that Nugent set were pressed high, based as they were on the capabilities of an independent wheelchair user. The effect when they were applied to new buildings across America was a massive leap, a huge extension of the accommodation parameters of public and employment buildings. The same occurred in Britain with the introduction of the Part M building regulation in 1987.

Notionally, the for-the-disabled Part M regulation could be reconstituted as a 'for everyone' access standard and come with prescriptions aimed at dealing with architectural discrimination against women and other building users as well as disabled people. But the for-the-disabled status of the Part M regulation is solidly entrenched, and exclusive concern with the accessibility needs of disabled people will be further reinforced with the full enforcement in 2004 of Part III of the Disability Discrimination Act.

In the context of extending the accommodation parameters of normal provision in buildings, the leap that Britain has made with Part M would not, we may observe, have been accomplished had America not set the agenda. As has been noted, universal design cannot be regulated. But as America demonstrated, access for the disabled could be regulated, and Britain followed suit. And in the cause of advancing the process of universal design the regulatory requirements that Part M has brought with it could hardly have been bettered.

The Part M building regulation is the base from which the prospects for implementing the precepts of universal design are considered. It is reviewed at this point in the context of public and employment buildings, and for these there are two relevant functions – visitability and employability. Broadly, accommodation parameters need to be extended further for the visitability purpose than the employability purpose. For a public building that will be visited by all kinds of disabled people they ought desirably, with reference to the universal design pyramid shown in diagram **1.1**, to embrace all those from level 1 up to and including level 8. Correspondingly for employability they ought in the case of buildings where wheelchair users could be employed to embrace all up to and including level 6, and up to and including level 5 in the case of buildings where ambulant disabled people might be employed but not wheelchair users, for example cafes, restaurants, petrol service stations and certain industrial manufacturing premises.

The requirements of the Part M regulation do not discriminate between public areas of a building and areas used only by staff employed in a building. They are, however, prescribed in the terms 'reasonable provision shall be made for disabled people', with what might be reasonable being a matter to be determined according to circumstances.

The universal design precept is that the accommodation parameters of normal provision should be extended as far as can be, thereby minimising the need for special provision for people with disabilities. The query here is what is meant by 'normal' and what by 'special'. The need for special provision, we may observe, is a function of the accommodation parameters of normal provision, and rather than engaging in the problematical exercise of attempting to define what is normal, the helpful way out is to say that normal provision is any provision in a building other than that provided exclusively for disabled people, either disabled people in general or a particular group of them such as wheelchair users, deaf people or blind people.

Three tests may be applied to assess the reasonableness of such special provision as is proposed in the course of designing of a building. The first is that it will be of *genuine value* to the disabled people it is intended to benefit. The second is that it *does not inconvenience other users* of the building; this applies other than where the advantages it will have for its intended beneficiaries will outweigh the disadvantages caused to others, taking into account the prospective proportion of such beneficiaries among all users of the building and the value of the provision for them. The third is that it *is warranted*: as a rule it will not be if the need it is intended to serve could just as well or better have been served by suitable normal provision. Features of buildings that can be special for disabled people are considered against these criteria.

In tiered seating areas of buildings such as theatres, cinemas and sports stadia special places in the form of pens for wheelchair users may be appropriate to meet Part M requirements. In small cinemas, etc. where wheelchair spaces are rarely occupied, the preferred arrangement may be to have the spaces in places where fixed seating can readily be removed; this can avoid inconvenience to others when there is a heavy demand for available seats. The issue is discussed on page 90.

In public toilets in public buildings it is reasonable for there to be at least one special unisex facility, as required by Part M. Where the special facility has a peninsular layout as in diagram **7.52** on page 82, it may be appropriate for there to be Part M-type wheelchair-accessible toilets in adjoining male and female zones, and these, being available to others including those with an infant in a pushchair, will not be 'special'. In employment buildings and in toilets for staff in public buildings a unisex facility may be provided in male and female zones; available to others than wheelchair users it will not thus be 'special'. In a building such as a petrol service station where only one wc compartment for public use is provided, it may be in the form of a Part M unisex toilet and thus be normal for all users.

For the purposes of the initial 1987 Part M building regulation, disabled people were defined as those who needed to use a wheelchair for mobility or had a physical impairment that limited their ability to walk. The 1992 revision came with an extended mandate that covered people with impaired hearing or sight, and this definition was retained with the 1999 revision. With regard to blind people a provision advised in the 1999 approved document is that a stepped approach to a building should have a corduroy tactile surface on its top landing. But a related Part M requirement is for there to be handrails to steps and landings on an approach to a building, and as an information and warning cue for blind people these serve better than a tactile surface.

As well as the corduroy surface the 1999 approved document also shows blister tactile pavings in the form that in recent years has been laid at street crossings across the country. There is no substantive evidence which supports the proposition that these are necessary for blind people, whereas it is apparent that they can be troublesome, uncomfortable and sometimes hazardous for other street users. Given the estimate that only about one in 5000 of all adult people who use shopping centres is a blind person, the case for retaining the Part M advice that tactile pavings should be incorporated in and around buildings is slim – by all three criteria they fail the test for special provision that is reasonable.

As noted earlier, the Part M advice is that a passenger lift should have landing and car controls that are not less than 900 and not more than 1200 mm above floor level. There is here an example of the consequences of setting cut-off points for Part M design standards in a way that will suit wheelchair users, but can be inconvenient for standing adult people. The estimates drawn from the findings of the sanitary provision research project were that independent wheelchair users comprised about one in 20 of all wheelchair users who visit shopping centres, or about one in 10 000 of all the adult people who do. And while it may well be that wheelchair users who use lifts independently are more numerous, they will still be a very small proportion of all lift users.

The 1999 Part M approved document does not advise that where in a lift there are controls at between 900 and 1200 mm to suit independent wheelchair users there ought also to be others at say between 1400 and 1700 mm above floor level to suit standing adult people. The omission is understandable: Part M is called *Access and facilities for disabled people*, and its requirements do not purport to be

about provision which will satisfy everyone. Affected by Part M, the common practice in Britain is for controls in lifts to be placed only between 900 and 1200 mm above floor level. As with wash basins, there is no single fixing height at which lift controls can be placed so that they are convenient for all their users.

A related section of the 1999 Part M approved document covers wheelchair stairlifts such as that shown in diagram **6.28**, and wheelchair platform lifts such as that shown in diagram **6.27**. Where the provision of a passenger lift would be impractical, it would be reasonable, it says, to install a wheelchair stairlift to reach a 'unique facility', one that might for example consist of a small library gallery, a staff rest room or a training room. Here is a case of special provision that would seem not to be warranted; if it is reasonable for such unique facilities to be wheelchair-accessible they ought properly to be served by a normal passenger lift, and in a new building subject to Part M that ought not to be impractical.

With regard to exclusive provision for disabled people, the advice in the 1999 approved document is that the installation of a wheelchair platform lift would be reasonable to effect a change of level within a storey in a new building where a ramped change was not practical. As a rule, this special provision would be reasonable – it is of a kind that is more commonly justified when alterations are made to existing buildings.

Discussion is on pages 91–4 on the Part M requirement that in a new hotel building one guestroom out of every 20 should be suitable for a wheelchair user in terms of size, layout and facilities. As is suggested there, a room suitable and convenient for disabled people in a new hotel does not need to be more spacious than other comparable rooms, and such for-the-disabled rooms will not be exclusive – as a rule they can equally well be used by people who are not disabled.

As has already been made clear, the implementation in practice of the precepts of universal design cannot be effected by regulatory control in the form of a building regulation. It has to be promoted by publicising its worth, and by encouragement and exhortation. In this endeavour the lead role could be with local authorities, using the scope they have for effecting change through the exercise of their planning and building control duties.

Many local authorities issue planning guidance on access provision for people with disabilities, and with it could come guidance on universal design. Usually they also have an access officer who is consulted when proposals are submitted for planning permission that cover accessibility issues; as a rule he or she is either in the planning or building control department. At that stage there is the opportunity to review proposals in the light of universal design, and to advise the architect and developer of how proposed access provision could be enhanced. Consideration could be given where relevant to public toilets, with a view for example of avoiding discrimination in the way that women would be treated, of making normal wc compartments convenient for all their users, and of having unisex facilities that are more spacious than the Part M standard. Relatedly, checks could be made on circulation spaces in respect of accessibility for electric scooter users and double-pushchair users. Similarly, the concerns of ambulant disabled people could be considered, with regard for example to the gradient of stairs and the provision of handrails.

Regarding alterations to existing buildings, there is uncertainty at the time this is written (September 2000) about the terms of such official guidance as might be issued for meeting the requirements of the Disability Discrimination Act. But material alterations to existing buildings will continue to be subject to building control approval; when they are assessed those that have an accessibility component could be considered with regard to their suitability for people with disabilities.

New housing

When architects design public buildings they treat the potential users of them collectively. As best they can, they attempt to make them conveniently usable by various different kinds of people, including those with disabilities. Housing is different; architects who design new houses usually have a brief for the kind of people they are intended for, and they can plan them to suit those who might be expected to live in them. The houses whose plans are shown on pages 106–10 are all social housing units built by housing associations, the type of housing that architects most frequently find themselves dealing with. In any new housing development built by a housing association most of the units will be for general needs, but among them a proportion – perhaps 5 or 10 per cent – will be wheelchair units, ones that with increased space standards are designed to be suitable for wheelchair users and other disabled people to live in.

The discussion on universal design has so far concentrated on public buildings, with two concepts being relevant in respect of how they are designed to be convenient for all their users. One is visitability, that they should be accessible to and usable by the people who visit them as members of the public. The other is employability, that they should be accessible to and usable by the staff who work in them. Correspondingly the relevant concepts that come with the design of new housing are livability, that new houses should be convenient for the people who will live in them, and visitability, that they should be accessible to relatives, friends and neighbours who come visiting.

It was visitability and private sector housing which in the 1980s prompted the initiative that led to the Part M building regulation being extended to cover new housing. Low-cost private sector housing, typically in the form of a two-storey box, has over the years been commonly designed to lesser space standards than those applied by local authorities and housing associations on the public sector side. In the 1980s it was unrealistic to suppose that speculative developers could be asked to provide housing suitable for disabled people to live in, but visitability was perhaps more readily achievable.

In the early 1980s there were disabled people who expressed concern that while their own homes were fully accessible and could be visited by all their friends, they were not able to visit their friends because their houses were not accessible. In 1985 the issue was taken up by the Prince of Wales' Advisory Group on Disability. With the backing of the National House-Building Council, private sector housebuilders were encouraged to plan their new developments to visitability standards, and advances were made. It was apparent, however, that only statutory regulations would oblige housebuilders to make visitability a feature of their new housing schemes.

The government was subjected to increasing pressure from disabled people and their organisations to extend Part M to cover new housing, and in 1997, Nick Rainsford, Minister for Housing and Construction in the new Labour government, responded positively. Encouraged among others by the Joseph Rowntree Foudation and leading housing associations, his policy line was that visitability controls – including the vital matter of a downstairs wc in all two-storey houses – should be applied to all new housing, not only the large family houses that private sector housebuilders had supposed might be affected.

With requirements for all new housing, the new-style Part M came into operation in October 1999. Its approved document detailed how its requirements would be applied. Other than where plot gradients exceeded 1:15, the entrances to all new dwellings would have to be wheelchair-accessible. Internally, habitable rooms on the entrance storey had to be wheelchair-accessible, along with a wc, the design conditions for which are set out in Chapter 7 on page 75. The relevant requirement, M3(1), reads 'Reasonable provision shall be made in the entrance storey of a dwelling for sanitary conveniences, or where the entrance storey contains no habitable rooms, reasonable provision for sanitary conveniences shall be made in either the entrance storey or a principal storey.' In this connection M3(2) reads

'"entrance storey" means the storey which contains the principal entrance to the dwelling, and "principal storey" means the storey nearest to the entrance storey which contains a habitable room, or if there are two such storeys equally near, either such storey.'

A notable feature of the Part M housing regulation is that its requirements are all for normal provision; it does not, as with public buildings, require any supplementary provision to be made which is special for people with disabilities.

Examples of two-storey houses built in accord with Part M requirements are shown on page 107. The plan diagrams on page 106 show ground floor flats. The general needs flats (diagrams **9.1a**, **9.2** and **9.3b**), while not being spacious, are suitable for most disabled people to live in. The wheelchair units (diagrams **9.1b** and **9.3a**) have more generous circulation spaces and larger bathrooms, and illustrate how universal design can be pressed further with the space standards that come with wheelchair housing as against general needs housing.

In parallel with the move towards the Part M regulation, the important advance during the 1990s was the successful promotion by the Joseph Rowntree Foundation of the concept of Lifetime Homes, the principle that houses should be designed to meet the needs of their occupiers throughout their lifetime. The commentary on page 104 describes Lifetime Homes in more detail, and plan examples are on pages 108 and 109. A feature of them is the allowance made for a through-floor lift to be installed should it be needed. In this regard the examples of two-storey wheelchair houses on page 110 are instructive; they demonstrate that the through-floor lift condition is better achieved by incorporating storerooms on both floors in which a lift can be placed if needed. In the context of universal design they show, as do the wheelchair flats on page 106, that designing to meet the needs of wheelchair users is advantageous.

On the move towards universal design the Part M housing regulation, like its public buildings counterpart, is now serving to substantially extend the accommodation parameters of normal provision. And Lifetime Homes, while not being a concept that could be nationally regulated, demonstrate most markedly the benefits that come with adherence to the precepts of universal design.

2 Building users: mobility equipment

Ambulant disabled people

The figures of ambulant disabled people shown in **2.1** are tall men. The spaces shown for them are for forward movement, although in practice ambulant people such as these are as a rule able with their mobility aids to turn to the side to negotiate narrow openings. In the context of universal design they do not therefore have the same significance as for example wheelchair users, pushchair users or electric scooter users, and they are comfortably accommodated by circulation spaces suitable for independent wheelchair users.

Self-propelled wheelchairs

In Britain it has since the early 1960s been the rule that a standard self-propelling wheelchair has main wheels at the rear and castor wheels at the front. Other standard features of the kind of wheelchair shown in **2.2** are pneumatic tyres, detachable armrests, swing-away detachable footrests that are adjustable in height, tipping levers at the rear and a folding cross-brace. The height of the centre of the seat is typically at about 470 mm above floor level, but most wheelchair users place a cushion on the seat, and the seat height indicated in the anthropometric diagrams on pages 28 and 29 is 490 mm.

Wheelchairs of this kind may have domestic armrests (**2.9**), allowing the user to approach closer to tables, wash basins etc. than where the armrests are as in **2.2**.

Attendant-pushed wheelchairs

The wheelchair shown in **2.4** has fixed armrests, fixed footrests, pneumatic rear wheels diameter 310 mm and solid front castor wheels diameter 205 mm. A similar chair known as a car transit wheelchair has detachable armrests, swing-away detachable footrests that are adjustable in height and a fold-down back.

In and around public buildings the wheelchairs that people use more often have large rather than small wheels; wheelchair users who are seen being pushed along streets in wheelchairs with large main wheels as in **2.2** may be able to move around independently inside buildings.

The reclining wheelchair shown in **2.5** has elevated legrests and a fully reclining back. As depicted its length is about 1300 mm, but this may be around 1750 mm where the backrest has been lowered and the legrests raised to the horizontal in order to accommodate a recumbent person.

Powered wheelchairs

Examples of powered wheelchairs are shown in **2.6** and **2.7**. In and around public buildings, small powered wheelchairs comparable to **2.7** are more commonly seen than large powered chairs. A small powered chair may have length and width dimensions of the order of 890 × 630 mm, a large one 1170 × 680 mm.

The gradient of a ramp that a powered wheelchair can be driven up is a function of the weight of the disabled person seated in it. As a general rule a typical powered chair can manage a 1:5 gradient without difficulty. The typical powered chair currently manufactured is designed to carry a weight of 115 kg (18 stone), with the heavy-duty chairs that are available being able to carry a weight of 165 kg

(26 stone). There can be a danger of the chair tipping over backwards if it is driven up a ramp steeper than about 1:5.

Shower chairs

The mobile shower chair shown in **2.8** has a perforated seat for drainage and brakes on all four castor wheels.

Electric scooters

In Britain in recent years there has been a steady increase in the use by disabled people of electric scooters for mobility purposes. Many have found that with electric scooters they are more easily able to travel out around local streets and shops and visit friends. A related important factor has been the growth of Shopmobility schemes, of which there are now (September 2000) some 250 in towns and cities around the country, where pushed wheelchairs, powered wheelchairs and electric scooters are available on loan to visitors with disabilities who come to do their shopping.

The two scooters shown in **2.10** and **2.11** are examples of the kind of scooters used by Shopmobility schemes in the year 2000.

A feature of them, as shown by the diagrams on page 47 and noted on page 42, is that the turning space they require is considerably more than that for self-propelled or pushed wheel-chairs or child pushchairs. It ought not, however, to be assumed that the turning space dimensions shown in **5.22** and **5.23** on page 47 will remain reliable for the architect's purposes;

the design of features of electric scooters is continuingly being refined and improved, one of the effects of which may that the turning space needed by typical scooters in future years is less than as shown in **5.22** and **5.23**.

Large electric scooters can have lengths of the order of 1650 mm.

Child pushchairs

Buggy-type child pushchairs are shown in **2.12** and **2.13**. These are small easily foldable light-weight chairs of a kind convenient for taking on buses, and are typical of the type of pushchair commonly seen in shopping centres.

The **2.12** single buggy has a width of 480 mm, enabling it to pass through narrow doors, as relevant diagrams in this book show. The impression is, however, that consumer prefer-ences for child pushchairs are changing, with more comfortable, better upholstered and larger pushchairs now becoming more prevalent. The width of such pushchairs is greater, of the order of 550 or 650 mm, but for passing through door openings, etc. they need no more space than standard wheelchairs. The carrycot shown in **2.14** has a width of 590 mm, with traditional perambulators commonly being wider than this.

Correspondingly, many double pushchairs commonly seen in shopping centres are wider than the 815 mm of the buggy shown in **2.13**, with widths ranging up to more than 1000 mm. Commentary on door openings with regard to double pushchairs is on page 42, relevant plan diagrams being on pages 46 and 47.

Ambulant disabled people's aids
Commentary page 17

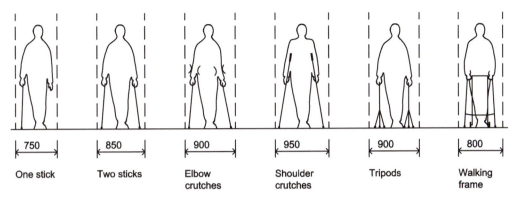

750	850	900	950	900	800
One stick	Two sticks	Elbow crutches	Shoulder crutches	Tripods	Walking frame

2.1 *Ambulant disabled people, utilisation space for forward movement*

Wheelchairs
Commentary page 17

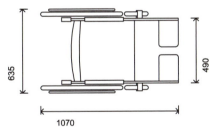

2.2 *Standard wheelchair. For a typical wheelchair of this kind the height above floor level of the top face of the handles is 920 mm and of the top face of the armrests 750 mm*

2.3 *Plan of standard wheelchair*

2.4 *Attendant-pushed wheelchair, width 635 mm, length 790 mm*

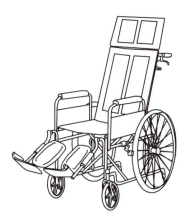

2.5 *Wheelchair with elevated legrests and reclining back, width 635 mm, length as shown is 1300 mm*

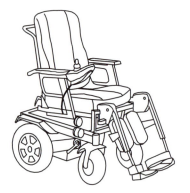

2.6 *Powered wheelchair, width 670 mm, length 1110 mm*

2.7 *Powered wheelchair, width 630 mm, length 990 mm*

2.8 *Shower chair, width 450 mm, length 450 mm*

2.9 *Domestic armrest on standard wheelchairs used to facilitate access to tables, etc.*

Electric scooters

Commentary page 18

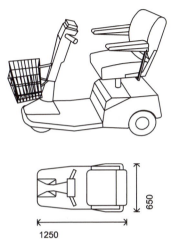

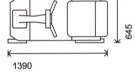

650

1250

2.10 *Three-wheel scooter*

645

1390

2.11 *Four-wheel scooter*

Child pushchairs

Commentary page 18

460

815

2.12 *Single buggy*

815

815

2.13 *Double buggy*

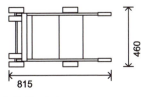

2.14 *Carrycot, width 590 mm, length 1060 mm*

3 Anthropometrics

The anthropometric data to the diagrams on pages 26–30 are derived from two sources. One is Henry Dreyfuss Associates' *The Measure of Man and Woman – Human Factors in Design*, published in 1993. The other is the second edition of Stephen Pheasant's *Bodyspace*, subtitled *Anthropometry, Ergonomics and the Design of Work,* published in 1998.

Dreyfuss

Henry Dreyfuss's 1993 book is the updated sequel to his 1960 landmark book, *The Measure of Man,* acknowledged around the world as the authoritative textbook of anthropometric data for architects, engineers and designers.

Dreyfuss's expertise was in the field of psychology, engineering, anthropology and physiology. With the coming of World War II he was commissioned by the US Department of Defense to develop human engineering standards for the design of military equipment, and in order to obtain relevant anthropometric data for the project he undertook a survey of a large sample of adult males in military service or suited for it. It was primarily the findings of that survey which informed the presentation of the series of anthropometric diagrams in the 1960 book.

Homogeneous populations and percentile measures

In studying a population of adult males who were servicemen, Dreyfuss had a homogeneous population, which enabled him to present comprehensive anthropometric data systematically. With stature being the key item, the body measurements of a homogeneous population when analysed are found to have a statistically normal distribution, meaning that when heights are plotted against incidence the graphical outcome is a symmetrical bell curve. On the left side of the bell are the 50 per cent of the population whose heights are below average, and on the right side the 50 per cent who are above average height. At the top centre of the bell is the mean average, the 50th percentile. Standard deviations, indices of the degree of variability in the population concerned, can then be calculated to measure the position of percentiles towards the low and high ends of the curve, for example the 5th percentile which indicates the height measure below which there are 5 per cent of the population – correspondingly there are 5 per cent above the 95th percentile. A common practice when applying anthropometric data to design considerations is to employ the central range from the 5th to the 95th percentiles, the effect of which is that 10 per cent of the population are ignored, meaning that in respect of heights tall and short people are excluded.

The measures of tall and short people

In the 1976 edition of *Designing for the Disabled,* the anthropometric diagrams, derived from Dreyfuss's 1960 book, were shown with 5th, 50th and 95th percentiles, and in early drafts of diagrams for this book the same practice was followed, again relying principally on Dreyfuss's data. But what became apparent when the Chapter 4 diagrams for the height of building fixtures were being drafted was that the 5th percentile did not sensibly represent short people, and nor did the 95th represent tall people. That might have been predicted, owing to short and tall men having been disregarded for the purposes of Dreyfuss's 1940s project on equipment for military personnel.

For representing short and tall people for universal design purposes, 1st and 99th percentile figures are much more appropriate than 5th and 95th. In this regard Dreyfuss's 1993 update of his 1960 book was informative; in place of 5, 50 and 95, the anthropmetric measures it presents are for 1, 50 and 99, and it was with reference to these that relevant diagrams for this book were redrafted. Queries remained, however, about the reliability of Dreyfuss's data; one of the concerns was that in the 1993 book the 50th percentile for the stature of adult men continued to be shown at 1755 mm as it had been in the 1960 book, this being a measure that had come from a survey made in the 1940s.

Stephen Pheasant's data
The suspicion was that for adult men in Britain in the twenty-first century, an average height of 1755 mm (5 ft 9 in) could be an underestimate, although perhaps a slight one. Confirmation came from an examination of the series of tables presenting detailed anthropometric estimates in Stephen Pheasant's 1998 book *Bodyspace* – ones derived from a range of surveys undertaken in Britain and elsewhere in recent years.

For British adults aged 19 to 65 the Pheasant estimate for the 50th percentile measure of the stature of men is 1740 mm. This is with unshod feet; with 25 mm added for the kind of everyday shoes that men wear, this becomes 1765 mm (5 ft 9½ in) in place of Dreyfuss's 1755 mm.

For the stature of women the corresponding 50th percentile Pheasant measure is 1610 mm; with 10 mm flat shoes the average height of women becomes 1620 mm and with 100 mm high-heel shoes 1710 mm. In **3.3** and related diagrams in Chapter 4 the add-on heel height is assumed to be 40 mm, giving an average height of 1650 mm (5 ft 5 in) in place of Dreyfuss's 1625 mm (5 ft 4 in).

In relevant diagrams in Chapter 4 a 'tall' person is placed at the 99th percentile and a 'short' person at the 1st. With reference to the stature of able-bodied men, **3.1** illustrates the issues involved. The normal distribution curve, drawn to scale on the x and y axes, shows the sharp inclines there are between around the 1st percentile and the 5th, and between around the 95th and the 99th. The 99th, at 1930 mm, indicates that 1 adult man in 100 is taller than 6 ft 4 in; the 50th, at 1765 mm, that the average height of an adult man is 5 ft 9½ in; and the 1st, at 1600 mm, that 1 adult man in 100 is shorter than 5 ft 3 in.

In recording anthropometric data, head height is the key item, and average measures of other bodily characteristics may not have equally neat statistical correspondences. Diversity is the rule. During adult life bodily changes occur within any individual and among groups of comparable individuals. People in different geographical areas, types of employment or social groups develop in different ways, and among people in different ethnic groups there are distinctively different bodily characteristics.

Elderly people and children
As people become older they diminish in size; the elderly woman shown in **3.4** is some 6 per cent smaller than the younger woman shown

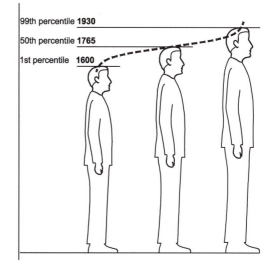

99th percentile **1930**
50th percentile **1765**
1st percentile **1600**

3.1 *Stature of able-bodied man*

in **3.3**. Relevant data are drawn from Dreyfuss and Pheasant, both of whom assume the population of elderly people has a statistically normal distribution.

The data for standing children (**3.5** and **3.6**) are derived from both Dreyfuss and Pheasant – their relevant data show no significant differences.

Ambulant disabled people

In respect of ambulant disabled people who are users of public buildings, no reliable anthropometric data could be obtained and then presented in the systematic form of **3.2–3.4**. A relevant factor is that there can be no generally respectable operational definition of the point at which ambulant disabled people can be distinguished from normal able-bodied people and therefore no means of assembling a meaningful sample of the population of ambulant disabled people.

It is also highly improbable that a cohort of ambulant disabled people, however selected, could be gathered which when measured for any particular anthropometric characteristic would be found to display a statistically normal distribution. There would be a skewed distribution, one where the modal average was for example at the 40th or 45th rather than the 50th percentile point. Skewed distributions have a place in anthropometric studies, but for the purposes of illustrating universal design it is advantageous to draw on populations whose anthropometric measures can reasonably be assumed to have a statistically normal distribution, permitting the position of percentiles either side of the central modal average to be calculated, including the important 1st and 99th.

The variability of wheelchair users

The issue of skewed versus normal statistical distributions affects any examination of wheelchair users. In the context of the usage of public buildings their anthropometric characteristics are so immensely variable that no representative sample of them could be expected to present a statistically normal distribution for any anthropometric measure.

A complicating factor is the variability of usage by wheelchair users of different types of public buildings. The profile of the population of wheelchair users who go to churches is, for example, very different from that of those who go to pubs. Diversity would similarly be found between the users of cafes and cinemas, or between theatres and swimming pools. An unavoidable effect of this is that, in whatever way a cohort of wheelchair users might be assembled for anthropometric study, none could reliably serve to represent the users of each and every type of public building.

In the case of wheelchair users who are employed in office-type buildings, a representative sample could well be statistically more homogeneous than a sample of the users of public buildings. But the application of anthropometric methodology to them could still pose intractable problems.

At issue is the definition of a wheelchair user. A reasonable premise might be that in respect of the usage of public buildings, a wheelchair user could be defined as someone who happened to be seated in a wheelchair when observed in the neighbourhood of a shopping centre. A representative sample of these could be obtained by enlisting all those who happened to be around on a typical shopping day. As is confirmed by the research findings reported on page 9, it would then be predictable to find that one segment of them was people who could get up and walk about unaided, another was people who could walk a short way with a handrail to hold onto, another was people able to stand to transfer from the wheelchair to a seat alongside, and another, a smaller segment, was people who were effectively chairbound, having no mobility function in their legs. In this connection the research findings set out in Table 1.2 on page 10 are relevant.

Independent wheelchair users

A suggested line of inquiry might be to study independent wheelchair users, with those eligible on the public buildings usage front being those who regularly travelled from home independently, propelled themselves around independently, and managed independently when using restaurants, banks, railway stations, swimming pools, hotels and other types of public buildings. Methodologically, any such inquiry would be hazardous.

The reference at this point is to diagrams in this book showing a person in a wheelchair who could be non-ambulant and able independently to do what the diagram shows them doing. Relevant examples are on pages 34, 37, 38 and 39. The characteristic that all these notional wheelchair users might be assumed to have in common is unimpaired upper limbs, since for all the tasks that are being performed in the diagrams a person confined to a wheelchair would need to have function in their arms and hands in order to accomplish the task.

By no means all of them might be as capable of undertaking the task concerned as a typical able-bodied person would be when placed in a wheelchair, though some might well be better able to. We may, however, imagine that they are able-bodied people who have been told to sit in a wheelchair and demonstrate what they can do.

Looking at the diagrams which show a wheelchair user in elevation, for example **4.11e**, **4.12c**, **4.14**, **4.17c**, **4.18**, **4.21** and **5.31**, the inference which follows is that in practice a real chair-bound person placed in any of the situations concerned would in effect be little or no less able to manage than the putative able-bodied person. Collectively therefore, in the context of anthropometric illustrations in diagrammatic form, it is admissible for normal able-bodied people to be surrogates for these wheelchair users.

The effect of this is that independent wheelchair users can be represented by able-bodied people who are placed in wheelchairs in respect of whichever of the activities shown in the seven itemised diagrams is concerned, along with others comparable to them. This affords a key to presenting anthropometric data for independent wheelchair users; relevant anthropometric data for seated normal able-bodied people can justifiably be employed.

It is on this basis that **3.7** and **3.8** are presented, with measurement data for seated people being drawn from Dreyfuss and Pheasant sources, and in certain circumstances modified by data which informed the wheelchair user anthropometric diagrams in the 1976 edition of *Designing for the Disabled*. For the proposed revision of the BS 5810 code of practice, *Access for the Disabled to Buildings*, an anthropometric study of wheelchair users has been made by Robert Feeney Associates of Loughborough, but at the time this is written (September 2000) a report on its methodology and findings has not yet been published.

Ambulant people
Commentary page 22

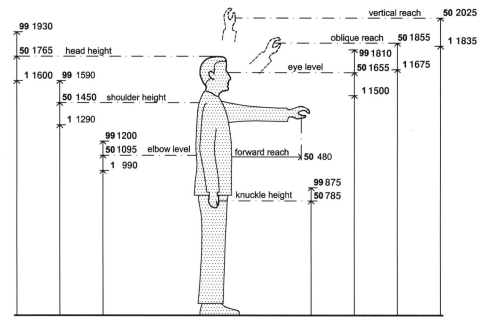

3.2 *Able-bodied men age 18–60*

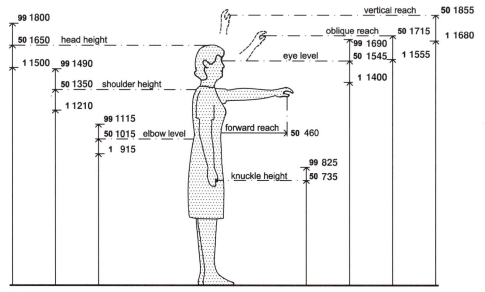

3.3 *Able-bodied women age 18–60*

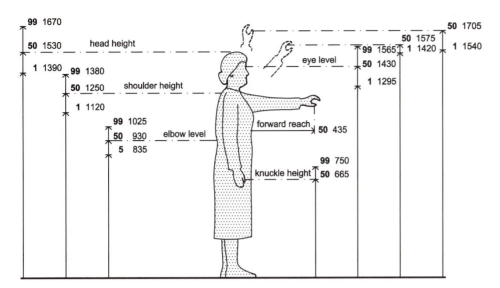

99 1670
50 1530   head height
1 1390   **99** 1380
50 1250   shoulder height
1 1120
99 1025
50 930   elbow level
5 835

50 1705
50 1575
99 1565   **1** 1420   **1** 1540
50 1430
1 1295

eye level

forward reach   **50** 435

knuckle height   **99** 750
50 665

3.4 *Elderly women age 60+*

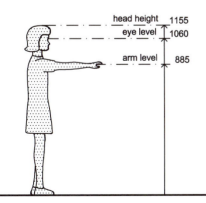

head height   1155
eye level   1060
arm level   885

3.5 *Children age 6*

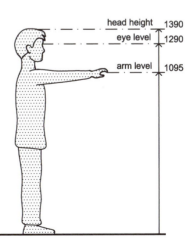

head height   1390
eye level   1290
arm level   1095

3.6 *Children age 10*

Wheelchair users
Commentary page 24

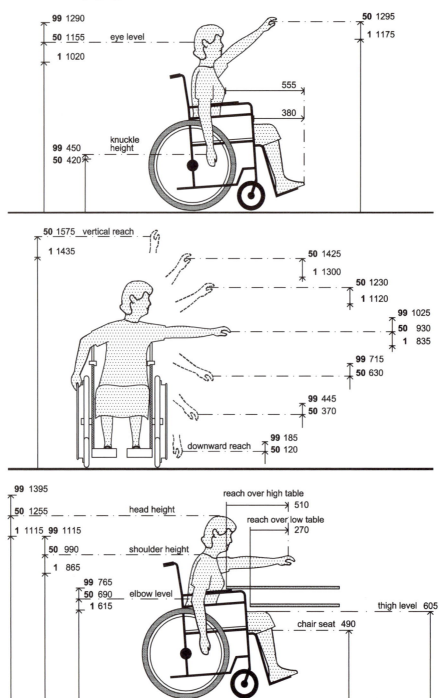

3.7 *Wheelchair users, women with unimpaired upper limbs*

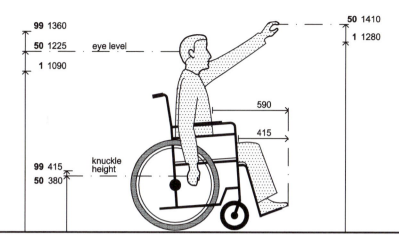

99 1360

50 1225   eye level

1 1090

50 1410

1 1280

590

415

99 415   knuckle
50 380   height

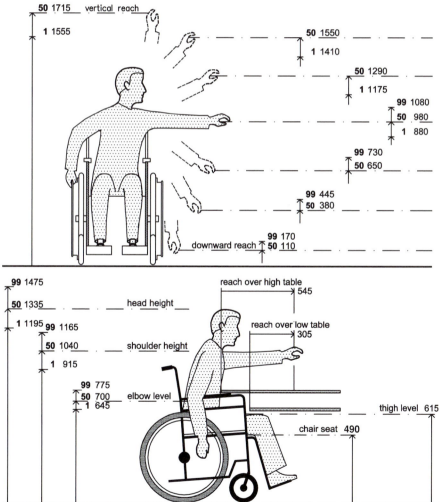

50 1715   vertical reach

1 1555

50 1550

1 1410

50 1290

1 1175

99 1080
50 980
1 880

99 730
50 650

99 445
50 380

99 170
downward reach   50 110

99 1475

50 1335   head height

1 1195   99 1165

50 1040   shoulder height

1 915

reach over high table
545

reach over low table
305

99 775
50 700   elbow level
1 645

thigh level   615

chair seat   490

3.8 *Wheelchair users, men with unimpaired upper limbs*

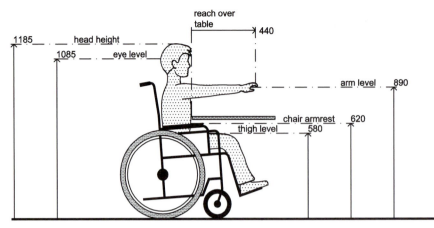

3.9 *Wheelchair users, 10-year-old children*

Seated women

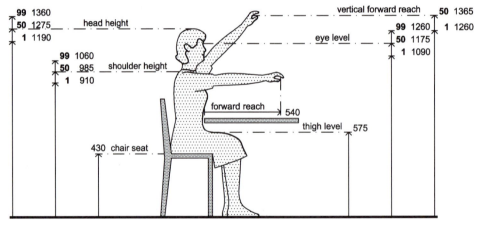

3.10 *Women age 18–60*

4 Heights of fixtures and fittings

As has been noted in Chapter 1, the height of fixtures and fittings in buildings poses problems for which universal design cannot always present satisfactory answers, for example where there are conflicting interests between children and adult people, and between standing people and wheelchair users.

The majority of the diagrams on pages 26–30 incorporate representations of standing people or wheelchair users who are using building fixtures and fittings. The dimensions associated with these figures, for example head height, eye level and arm reaches, are derived from the anthropometric data in the diagrams on pages 26–30.

Doors and windows
Diagrams **4.1**, **4.2** and **4.3** are self-explanatory.

Mirrors
A fixed wall mirror with bottom edge at 750 mm and top edge at 1850 mm above floor level (**4.4**) gives a full view of face and clothing for all standing people and wheelchair users.

For face-grooming, a mirror with the bottom edge at 1200 mm serves standing people, including short elderly women (eye level at around 1300 mm above floor level) and also children aged about nine or over as indicated in **3.5** and **3.6**.

As shown in **4.5**, a tilting mirror on a dressing table or other surface can be convenient for all users.

Wcs
In public toilets, wcs in male and female areas normally have the seat at about 405 mm (**4.6**), which is not inconvenient for normal able-bodied people. For wheelchair users and other disabled people, whether in special unisex toilets or elsewhere, research findings indicate that a wc seat at about 475 mm (**4.7**) is appropriate[1], and is advised in the 1999 Part M Approved Document.

Urinals
The realisation of universal design can pose awkward problems where bowl urinals are to be provided. In a public toilet facility that has a single bowl urinal there is no level at which it can be fixed so that it will conveniently serve both tall men and small boys, the problem being illustrated by **4.8**.

Where bowl urinals are to serve adult men only, as may happen for example in staff toilets in employment buildings, bowl rims may reasonably be between 550 and 600 mm; this compares with the average height of 630 mm in typical public toilet facilities in Britain.

In public toilets that serve both men and boys, urinal bowl rims at 600 mm for men and 300 mm for boys can be suitable, as shown in **4.9**. The suggested 300 mm for boys compares with the average rim height of 510 mm of urinals for boys placed alongside those for men in typical public toilets in Britain; as **4.8c** and **d** show, 510 mm is too high for small boys to manage.

The alternative is stall urinals, as shown in **4.10**. Diagram **4.10c** shows a wheelchair user who can stand to transfer onto a platform, which as shown is at 140 mm above floor level; where there is a platform such as this it can be helpful for ambulant disabled people if a grab rail is fixed to the wall in the position shown. Where practicable it is preferable for disabled users for the platform to be level with the floor, without a step up.

Wash basins

In buildings of all kinds where there are sanitary facilities, a common circumstance is that a single wash basin has to serve all users. In domestic housing the condition occurs in bathrooms and wc compartments; in hotels it occurs in the bathrooms of guest suites, and similarly it occurs in many small public buildings where wc compartments incorporate a wash hand basin.

In spacious cloakrooms in public and office buildings in Britain there is, according to circumstances, a row or rows of two, three or more wash basins. The standard practice is that these are all at the same level.

In Britain the average height at which wash basins are fixed is with the bowl rim at 820 mm above floor level. For standing adults, including tall men (**4.11a**) and average-height women (**4.11b**), this is inconveniently low; a rim level at 950 mm (**4.11c** and **d**) or even higher is preferable. But for small children a basin with its rim at 820 mm (**4.11f**) is not easy to reach and use conveniently. For wheelchair users an 820 mm rim height is about as satisfactory as can be, whether the basin is approached frontally as in **4.11e** or laterally as shown in **7.68** on page 86.

It is neither reasonable nor practicable to advocate that all wash basins in all situations should be adjustable in height, and in the context of universal design there is an insoluble problem – there is no level at which a wash basin can be placed to suit all users.

Hand dryers

As **4.12** indicates, hand dryers with the warm air blower at 1100 mm above floor level will generally serve adult people, children and wheelchair users.

Lift controls

With regard to suiting all users, the placing of lift controls can present problems owing to the conflict of interest between independent wheelchair users and normal able-bodied people.

The 1999 Part M Approved Document advises that a wheelchair user needs sufficient time to manoeuvre into a lift, and within it should not be restricted for space and should be able to reach the controls which direct the lift. With the capabilities of independent wheelchair users thus being a paramount consideration, the Approved Document goes on to say that requirement M2 (that reasonable provision be made for disabled people) will be satisfied if a lift has landing and car controls which are not less than 900 mm and not more than 1200 mm above the landing and the car floor, at a distance of at least 400 mm from the front wall.

As **4.13** shows, the 900/1200 condition is not satisfactory for average-height adult people, for whom a vertical batch of controls in the range 1200 to 1700 mm above floor level would be more convenient. For a normal adult person who is visually handicapped (**4.15**), using controls in the 900/1200 range can be tiresome, as also it may be for ambulant disabled people who cannot stoop. For wheelchair users (**4.14**), 900 to 1200 mm is just about ideal, although 1100 to 1400 mm would not be significantly less easily managed, and would be reasonable for standing adult people.

To resolve the problem while adhering to the advice in the Part M approved document, a choice between suitably placed horizontal and vertical batches of controls (**4.16**) could satisfy all users.

Shelves

The use of shelves involves reaching for books, foodstuffs, kitchen equipment, supermarket goods, luggage or other items stored on them. Women are shown on relevant diagrams on page 39 because their range of reach is generally less than men's and therefore more apposite to universal design considerations.

Predictably, the diagrams on page 39 show that ambulant women can conveniently reach relatively high-level shelves that are beyond the reach of wheelchair users.

Wheelchair users cannot for example reach goods on typical 300 mm deep shelves that are above 900 mm high kitchen units, and in practice such shelves are commonly placed substantially higher than the point at about 1600 mm that an average-height woman can comfortably reach to take goods off them (**4.17d**).

Whatever height shelves may be above floor level, a wheelchair can as a rule more readily reach them where the approach is lateral (**4.17c**) rather than frontal (**4.17e**).

With regard to goods placed on shelves in public buildings, for example books in bookshops and canned foods in supermarkets, it would be not realistic to insist that all should be within the very limited range of reach of wheelchair users. Understandably, this is not a matter that the 1999 Part M Approved Document suggests should be subjected to the 'reasonable provision for disabled people' requirement.

Work surfaces and tables
With regard to work surfaces and tables there need not be a conflict between the needs of able-bodied people and wheelchair users. **4.18a–c** show a woman in a wheelchair who is writing. This is more comfortably undertaken where the work surface is at 700 mm above floor level (**4.18b**), although the range of reach may be more restricted than where access is available below an 800 mm surface (**4.18a**).

The alternative, one that independent wheelchair users may employ in public buildings where counters preclude frontal approach for writing purposes, is to approach the work surface laterally. As **4.18c** shows, writing tasks are manageable where the surface is at 650 mm above floor level. In banks, post offices and other public buildings such as hotel reception desks and at ticketing points in theatres, cinemas and railway stations, counters at which standing customers are served are commonly at about 950 mm above floor level. In such cases it may be practicable to insert a pull-out shelf which will permit either frontal or lateral wheelchair approach, and so enable wheelchair users to sign credit card slips, write cheques or check that the tickets they are given are in order.

Coded access panels
The digits on finger-press code panels, for example ones where the correct code will open doors, release money, produce tickets or raise car park barriers, may need to be legible from a distance, and for standing people it is preferable that they are not at low level. Diagrams **4.19** and **4.20** suggest that to serve both ambulant people and wheelchair users a height range between 1100 and 1400 mm above floor level may be appropriate.

Socket outlets
In **4.21** an independent wheelchair user is shown reaching socket outlets at 450 and 1200 mm above floor level; it is between these levels that the 1999 Part M approved document advises that socket outlets should be placed in new housing subject to the Part M regulation. As **4.22** shows, a wheelchair user cannot, or not without difficulty, reach a socket outlet on the back wall above a kitchen worktop.

Doors and windows
Commentary page 31

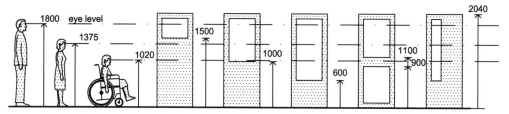

4.1 *Standard-panel glazed doors, sightlines. The figures represent tall ambulant men, short ambulant women and short wheelchair users*

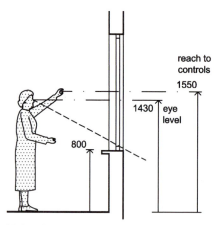

4.2 *Window. The figure represents average-height elderly women*

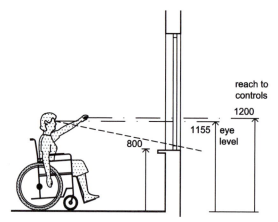

4.3 *Window. The figure represents average-height wheelchair user*

Mirrors
Commentary page 31

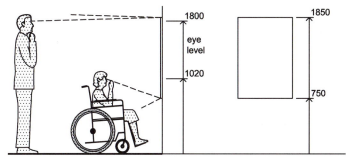

4.4 *Wall mirror. The figures represent tall ambulant men and short wheelchair users*

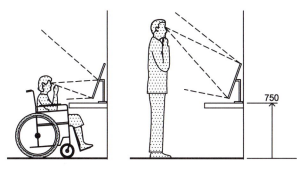

4.5 *Tilted mirror on dressing table. The figures represent short wheelchair users and tall ambulant men*

Wcs and urinals
Commentary page 31

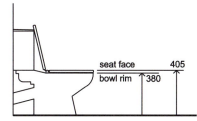

4.6 *Wc bowl, standard provision*

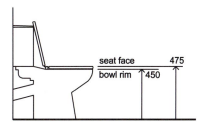

4.7 *Wc bowl for disabled people as advised in 1999 Part M Approved Document*

Urinals
Commentary page 31

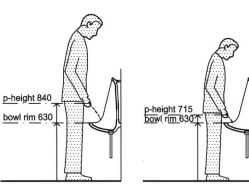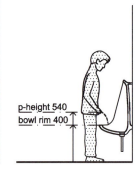

a *Tall man*　　**b** *Short man*　　**c** *Boy age 7*　　**d** *Boy age 4*

4.8 *Bowl urinals*

4.9 *Bowl urinals for boys and men*

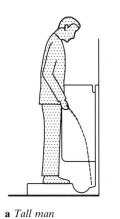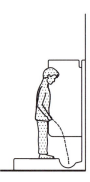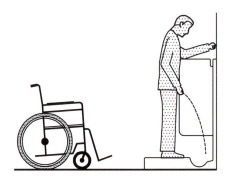

a *Tall man*　　**b** *Boy age 4*　　**c** *Ambulant wheelchair user*

4.10 *Stall urinals*

Wash basins and hand dryers
Commentary page 32

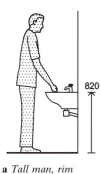

a *Tall man, rim at 820 mm*

b *Average-height woman, rim at 820 mm*

c *Tall man, rim at 950 mm*

d *Average-height woman, rim at 950 mm*

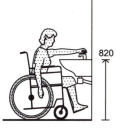

e *Wheelchair user, rim at 820 mm*

f *Child age 4, rim at 820 mm*

4.11 *Wash basins*

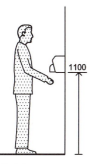

a *Average-height man*

b *Boy age 6*

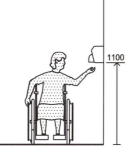

c *Wheelchair user*

4.12 *Hand dryers*

Lift controls
Commentary page 32

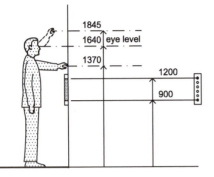

4.13 *Lift controls, average-height man. Panel to the right shows height conditions advised in 1999 Part M approved document*

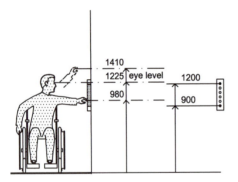

4.14 *Lift controls, wheelchair user*

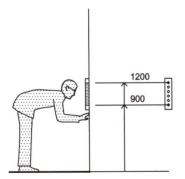

4.15 *Average-height man needing close view of lift control information*

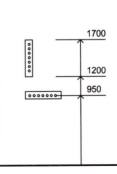

4.16 *Choice of lift control positions*

Shelves
Commentary page 33

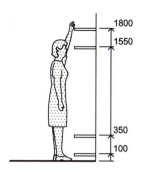

a *Average-height woman*

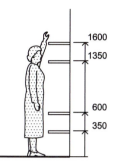

b *Short elderly woman*

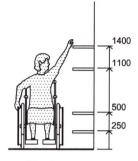

c *Wheelchair user, side reach*

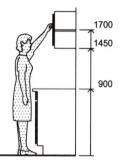

d *Average-height woman, reach over kitchen units 600 mm deep*

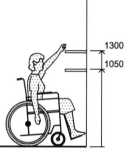

e *Wheelchair user, front reach*

4.17 *Reaches to shelves*

Work surfaces and tables
Commentary page 33

4.18a *Wheelchair user, frontal approach to work surface/table at 800 mm above floor level*

4.18b *Wheelchair user, frontal approach to work surface/table at 700 mm above floor level*

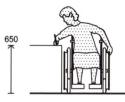

4.18c *Wheelchair user, lateral approach to counter/work surface at 650 mm above floor level where frontal access is prevented*

Coded access panels
Commentary page 33

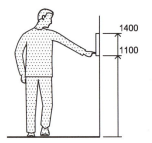

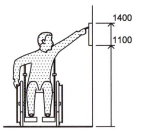

4.19 *Digital code panel, standing people*

4.20 *Digital code panel, wheelchair users*

Socket outlets
Commentary page 33

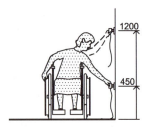

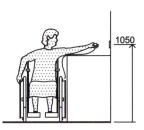

4.21 *Wheelchair user, access to sockets on unobstructed wall surfaces*

4.22 *Wheelchair user, reach towards sockets above kitchen worktop 900 mm high, 600 mm deep*

5 Horizontal circulation

Passing spaces

The passing spaces for wheelchair users and others that are shown in **5.1** are within standard passageway widths – 1200, 1500 or 1800 mm.

Straight approaches through openings

In **5.2–5.8**, minimum width openings are shown where the user's direct route to the opening is unobstructed.

As is shown in **5.3** and **5.4**, a typical independent wheelchair user is able to steer through a narrower opening than a person pushing an occupied wheelchair. The marked difference between a buggy-type double pushchair and a large double pushchair is shown in **5.5** and **5.6**.

Passing through doors

A standard BS 4787 900 mm internal timber doorset gives a clear opening width of 775 mm, as shown in **5.8**.

The standard 900 mm external timber doorset (**5.10**, **5.11a**) gives a clear opening width of 750 mm.

Where a weatherboard is fixed to an external timber door, the clear opening will be reduced at floor level. A 1000 mm doorset that has a weatherboard projecting 50 mm will give a clear opening width of 800 mm, instead of 850 mm where there is not a weatherboard (**5.11b**).

The 1999 Part M Approved Document advises a minimum clear opening width of 750 mm for internal doors and 800 mm for entrance doors.

For virtually all building users, opening and getting through doors in public buildings may pose problems, the only satisfactory arrangement being automatic-opening doors or, where regulations permit, doors that are held open with releasable catches.

To get through spring-loaded self-closing doors, most pushchair users and most pushers of wheelchairs need a third person to help, with most independent wheelchair users needing a second person.

A common practice in Britain is for double doors to be in 1500 mm openings, meaning that a single-pushchair user can pass through with one leaf held open, whereas wheelchair users and double-pushchair users need to have both doors held open, as shown in **5.13** and **5.14**.

In new construction or alterations to existing doorways an alternative may be for doorleafs to be offset, as shown in **5.15**.

In the case of doors opening into small rooms an option is a reduced-swing doorset of the kind shown in **5.16**.

Revolving doors may be unmanageable for pushchair users and wheelchair users, and hazardous to ambulant disabled people. An adjoining side door should be available, preferably an automatic-opening door (**5.17**).

Turning spaces

The turning spaces for wheelchair users, electric scooter users and pushchair users shown in **5.18–5.25** are based on a direct turn that is made without shunting. Utilisation spaces are shown for passing through a 775 or 875 mm door opening.

An independent wheelchair user can steer and turn his or her wheelchair more economically and accurately than the person who is pushing a loaded wheelchair; the comparisons are between **5.18** and **5.20**, and between **5.19** and **5.21**.

The scooter shown in **5.22** is of the type illustrated in **2.10** on page 21, found when tested to have a front wheel turn radius of 1900 mm. That shown in **5.23** is of the type illustrated in **2.11**, found when tested to have an outer front wheel turn radius of 2600 mm.

Other electric scooters may require less turning space, as noted on page 18.

A single buggy-type pushchair (**5.24**) can be turned from a 900 mm passageway through a 900 mm doorset 775 mm opening. A double buggy-type pushchair cannot pass through a 775 mm opening; diagram **5.25** shows an 875 mm opening as with a 1000 mm internal doorset.

Entrance lobbies and internal lobbies
Diagrams **5.26a**, **5.27a** and **5.28a** show lobby dimensions as advised in the 1999 Part M approved document for meeting Part M requirements for public buildings. The doorsets in these diagrams are 900 mm with 775 mm openings, i.e. as could be placed in internal lobbies rather than 1000/850 as might come with Part M-compliant external lobbies.

Diagrams **5.26b**, **5.27b** and **5.28b** show 1000 mm doorsets with 850 mm openings; these are needed for internal lobbies which cater for double-pushchair users.

The more spacious **b** lobbies are more manageable for building users generally, although the **a** spaces are suitable for independent wheelchair users.

For lobbies with double doors, the Part M examples (**5.29a** and **5.30a**) give restricted space for independent or pushed wheelchair users, the comparison being with the more spacious corresponding examples (**5.29b** and **5.30b**).

Approaches to doors
Where the approach to a door is head-on, an independent wheelchair user with unimpaired upper limbs in a standard wheelchair can reach forward to the door handle, pull the door open while reversing, and pass through (**5.31**).

The proviso here is that a wheelchair user may find it difficult or impossible to pull the door open while reversing if it has a spring-loaded hinge.

Turns by an independent wheelchair user through a 775 mm door opening from a 1200 mm passageway are shown in **5.32**. For independent wheelchair users **5.32a** is manageable, whereas **5.32b** is not; for a door which opens this way, utilisation space needs to be as in **5.32c**. The space needed by a wheelchair user who has to travel beyond a door that opens into the passageway is shown in **5.32d**.

As indicated by comparisons of relevant diagrams on page 47, more generous turning space is needed for a wheelchair user who is being pushed than by one who is propelling their own wheelchair. With some shunting the spaces in **5.32** are, however, manageable for a wheelchair pusher. Interestingly, there are instances here where an independent wheelchair user needs more space than a pushed wheelchair user; for the latter the extra space by the door handle in **5.32c** as compared with **5.32b** is not essential, and in respect of **5.32d**, assuming the door when opened folds back against the wall, the run-on space beyond the door swing is not essential.

The unobstructed space by the leading edge of a door
Although an independent wheelchair user with unimpaired upper limbs may be able to reach forward to the handle of a door directly in front of him or her (**5.31**), he or she is helped to open the door more easily if there is clear space to the side of it. A common recommendation is to have an unobstructed space on the side next to the leading edge of a door extending at least 300 mm; for a principal entrance door this is advised in the 1999 Part M approved document, and it is generally supposed that the 300 mm clear space effectively serves its purpose.

The appropriateness of the 300 mm condition is considered with reference to the **5.33** sequence of diagrams where there is a 300 mm wide space, as against the **5.34** sequence where the space is 600 mm wide.

5.33a shows that the 300 mm space is insufficient for the door swing to clear the side of the wheelchair without the wheelchair user needing to drive backwards while pulling the door open (**5.33b**) before he can pass through (**5.33c**). He cannot then easily turn to pull the door closed behind him (**5.33d**) and may have to find a place where he can turn his chair round and return (**5.33e**). In practice an independent wheelchair user is little better catered for with the 300 mm space than had they been negotiating their way through a 900 mm door from a 900 mm wide passageway.

With a 600 mm wide clear space by the door the movement is much easier; the wheelchair user can open the door without needing to reverse (**5.34a,b**), and when he has passed through he can turn to close the door (**5.34c,d**).

Where a door has a spring-loaded hinge it is much more difficult for a wheelchair user to pass through it, as in **5.33**, because he has to reverse while pulling it, than it is in **5.34** where there is sufficient space to avoid needing to reverse.

Backwards moves

The wheelchair user who needs help to move around is usually pushed in a forward direction. But for turning through doors at home and crossing the threshold at the front door, it is common practice for the helper to pull the wheelchair backwards, avoiding the tendency there is with assisted forward movement for the castor wheels to skew when they cross the threshold.

Where a turn has to be made in a confined space, it is also easier for the pusher to accurately and economically steer the wheelchair through a door opening where it is pulled backwards rather than pushed forward.

As shown in **5.35a**, a straight reverse move can be made through a 900 mm door with a 775 mm clear opening from a 900 mm passageway. The move is somewhat easier from a 1200 mm passageway (**5.35b**), and where a right angle turn has to be made the move is facilitated where there is a 1200 mm passageway (**5.35c**) rather than 1050 or 900 mm as permitted under the terms of Table 5.1.

Part M design standards

For wheelchair users to pass from passageways through doors the Part M design standards for public and employment buildings are more accommodating than those for new housing; for the former the minimum width advised for passageways is 1200 mm, whereas for the latter it is 900 mm.

Table 5.1 lists the minimum widths of doorways and passageways in new housing prescribed for the purposes of the 1999 Part M building regulation.

Part M housing, passageway and door widths

With regard to housing, **5.36** demonstrates the difficulty that a wheelchair user has when attempting to pass through the 775 mm opening of a 900 mm doorset from a 900 mm passageway. With 900 mm minimum passageway and an 800 mm door opening, **5.37**, reproduced from the 1999 Part M approved document, is virtually the same. The associated **5.38** diagrams confirm that this does not give convenient wheelchair accessibility, with the turning manoeuvres being demonstrably impracticable.

Thresholds

For new dwellings to comply with Part M, the 1999 approved document advice is that an accessible threshold should be provided where the approach to the entrance is level or ramped. The acceptable example shown in **5.39** involves a short ramp on the outside and a height of 10 mm above internal floor level, enough to make it sensible for many wheelchair users confronted by it to be pulled in and out backwards.

Table 5.1 Minimum widths of doorways and passageways in new housing needed to satisfy the requirements of the 1999 Part M building regulation

Doorway clear opening width	Passageway width
750 mm or wider	900 mm (when approach is head-on)
750 mm or wider	1200 mm (when approach is not head-on)
775 mm or wider	1050 mm (when approach is not head-on)
800 mm or wider	900 mm (when approach is not head-on)

Passing spaces
Commentary page 41

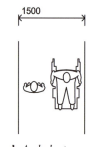

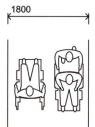

a *Ambulant person and single-pushchair user*

b *Ambulant person and independent wheelchair user*

c *Ambulant person and double-pushchair user*

d *Independent wheelchair user and pushed wheelchair user*

e *Double-pushchair user and pushed wheelchair user*

5.1 *Passing spaces*

Straight approaches through openings
Commentary page 41

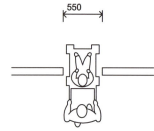
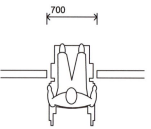
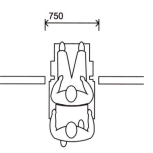

5.2 *Pushed single buggy-pushchair*

5.3 *Independent wheelchair user*

5.4 *Pushed wheelchair user*

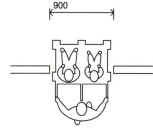
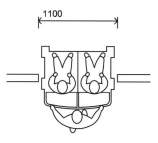
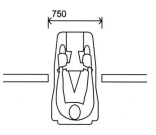

5.5 *Pushed double buggy-pushchair*

5.6 *Pushed large double pushchair*

5.7 *Electric scooter user*

Doors and door openings

Commentary page 41

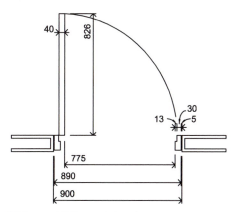

5.8 *Internal 900 mm timber doorset*

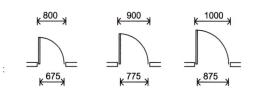

5.9 *Internal timber doorsets, clear opening widths*

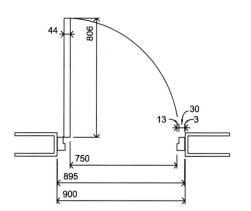

5.10 *External 900 mm timber doorset. A weatherboard fixed to the door may reduce the clear opening width*

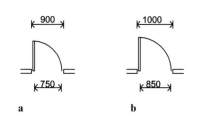

a   b

5.11 *External timber doorsets, clear opening widths*

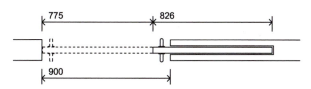

5.12 *Internal sliding door giving 775 mm clear opening*

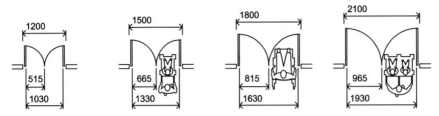

5.13 *Internal double-leaf timber doorsets. Lower set of dimensions are clear opening widths*

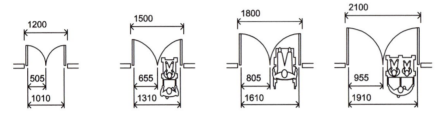

5.14 *External double-leaf timber doorsets. Lower set of dimensions are clear opening widths*

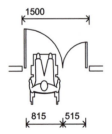

5.15 *Internal double-leaf doors offset*

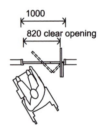

5.16 *Reduced-swing doorset*

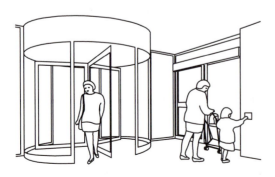

5.17 *Revolving door and automatic opening door*

Turning to pass through door openings

Commentary page 41

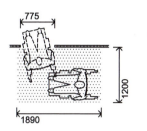

5.18 *Independent wheelchair user through 900 mm internal door. This accords with guidance for meeting Part M requirements*

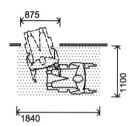

5.19 *Independent wheelchair user through 1000 mm internal door*

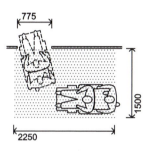

5.20 *Pushed wheelchair user through 900 mm internal door*

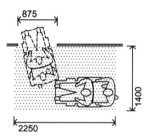

5.21 *Pushed wheelchair user through 1000 mm internal door*

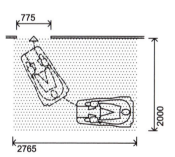

5.22 *3-wheel electric scooter user through 900 mm internal door*

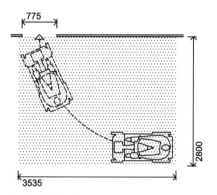

5.23 *4-wheel electric scooter user through 900 mm internal door*

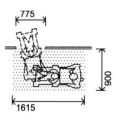

5.24 *Single buggy-pushchair through 900 mm internal door*

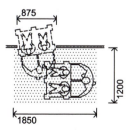

5.25 *Double buggy-pushchair through 1000 mm internal door*

Entrance lobbies and internal lobbies

Commentary page 42

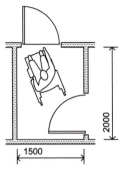

5.26a *Part M example*

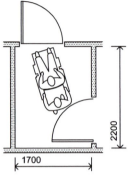

5.26b *Corresponding example*

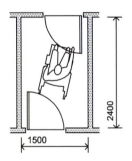

5.27a *Part M example*

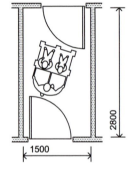

5.27b *Corresponding example*

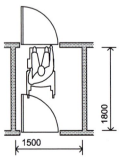

5.28a *Part M example*

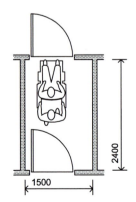

5.28b *Corresponding example*

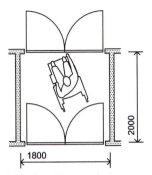

5.29a *Part M example*

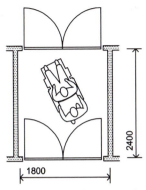

5.29b *Corresponding example*

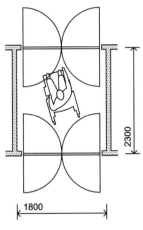

5.30a *Part M example*

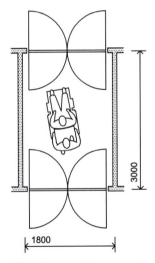

5.30b *Corresponding example*

Wheelchair users, movement through door openings
Commentary page 42

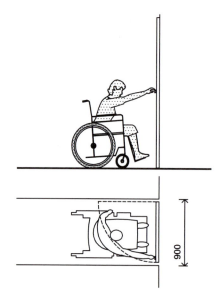

5.31 *Independent wheelchair user, forward reach to door handle*

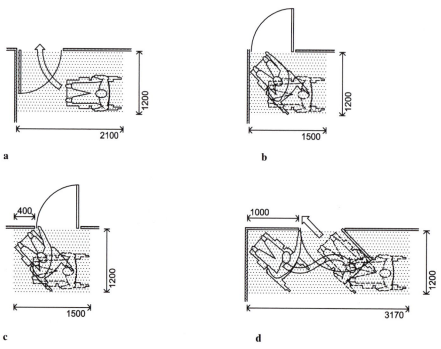

5.32 *Independent wheelchair users, turns through doors*

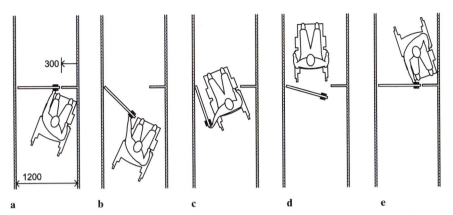

a   b   c   d   e

5.33 *Independent wheelchair user passing from 1200 mm passageway through 900 mm door with 300 mm clear space to the side*

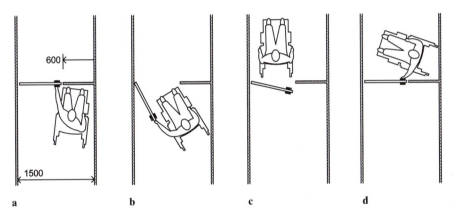

a   b   c   d

5.34 *Independent wheelchair user passing from 1500 mm passageway through 900 mm door with 600 mm clear space to the side*

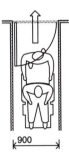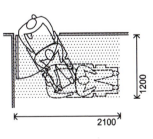

a *From 900 mm passageway through door* **b** *From 1200 mm passageway through door* **c** *Turning from 1200 mm passageway through door*

5.35 *Assistant pulling person in wheelchair backwards through door*

Housing, passageway spaces
Commentary page 43

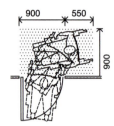

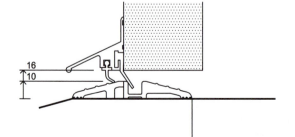

5.36 *Wheelchair turn from 900 mm passageway through 900 mm door, clear opening width 770 mm*

5.37 *Guidance in 1999 Part M Approved Document for passageways in Part M housing*

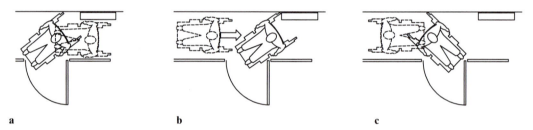

a   b   c

5.38 *Examples of difficulty turning wheelchair in arrangement advised for Part M purposes*

Thresholds
Commentary page 43

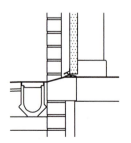

5.39 *Part M housing, example of low threshold*

6 Vertical circulation

Steps and stairs

The application of universal design to the planning of steps and stairs is illustrated in **6.1–6.3**. For all users, in particular ambulant disabled people, the broad principle is that the less steep the gradient of a stairway, the more comfortable it is to go up and down, and the less hazardous it is when going down. Relatedly the dimensional relationship between goings and rises has to give steps that are convenient to use.

The diagrams are indicative, being based on the principle that different design norms are appropriate for (i) external steps to buildings which may be vulnerable to rain, ice and snow, (ii) internal stairs in public buildings and (iii) stairways in domestic housing.

Rises and goings

For stepped approaches to public buildings, the advice in the 1999 Part M approved document is that rises should be not more than 150 mm and goings not less than 280 mm. For internal stairs in public buildings the advice is that rises should be not more than 170 mm and goings not less than 280 mm. For dwellings that are to comply with the Part M regulation, the advice for stepped approaches is that rises should be between 75 and 150 mm, with goings being not less than 280 mm.

Going-down hazards

A stairway user is more at risk of stumbling and falling when coming down stairs than going up, a relevant factor being the depth of treads. When climbing, a typical user places only part of the foot on the treads, whereas when descending the whole foot, or most of it, is placed on each tread. The narrower the tread, the more the user will twist the foot sideways when descending. With overall shoe lengths near to 300 mm not being uncommon, and recognising that ambulant disabled people need to place their leading foot securely on each tread as they descend a stairway, the going should desirably be not less than 300 mm for safety and convenience, and preferably of the order of 350 mm or more.

There are thus reservations to be expressed about the Part M advice that goings can be as short as 280 mm. For external steps **6.1** shows goings of 400, 450 and 500 mm, and for internal stairs in public buildings **6.2** shows goings of 300, 350 and 400 mm.

The Part K formula

As research findings have indicated, there is no definitive formula for 'correct' configurations of stair rises and goings[1]. For steps and stairs generally, the advice in the Part K building regulation approved document is that 2R + G (twice the rise plus the going) should be between 550 and 700 mm, which can entail unduly high rises and shallow goings. The steepest stair on page 58 (**6.3a**) scores 625, as do **6.3b** and **6.3c**. The least steep stair (**6.1c**) with its 500 mm goings and 110 mm rises scores 720.

Stairs in domestic housing

With the emphasis being on visitability rather than livability, the Part M regulation as it applies to housing does not cover stairs in new 2- or 3-storey housing.

In new housing (whether social housing or private sector) it is common for the floor-to-floor height to be 2700 mm. Relatedly it is common for there to be 13 stairs which in a straight flight give the 45° gradient shown in

6.3a. Particularly in low-cost private sector housing, it is not unusual to incorporate winders, with the gradient on the inside where the stair turns being close to 90°.

Within the same 2700 mm floor height as in **6.3a**, the comparison is with **6.3b** with its 15 stairs and **6.3c** with 17. Both of these come nearer to universal design, with the stairs being easier for elderly people, ambulant disabled people and pregnant women to manage, and for small children to be at less risk of falling and injuring themselves. The 307 mm goings that come with the **6.3c** stair allow handicapped and elderly people to place a foot securely on them when coming down.

Whether it be social housing or speculative private sector housing, a consideration which affects the planning of new houses is the maximisation of usable space in rooms such as living rooms, kitchens and bedrooms, a related effect being the need to minimise the space occupied by stairways. A stairway configuration as in **6.3a** is not good practice by the precepts of universal design, but it tends to be the norm. An effect of better practice, of having for example a stairway as in **6.3c**, is to substantially increase the floor area that the stairway occupies. For **6.3c** the dimension on plan from bottom to top risers is 4.91 m; for **6.3b** it is 3.71 m, and for **6.3a** 2.51 m. With straight flights the effect is that **6.3c** occupies 96 per cent more space than **6.3a**.

Handrails
A disabled person using a handrail when climbing stairs reaches forward with their arm, as shown in **6.4a**. At the head of the stairs they are helped if the handrail is extended so that they can use it to pull up the last two steps. For this purpose the horizontal dimension from the face of the top riser should preferably be not less than 600 mm (**6.4b**). The relevant diagram in the Part M approved document shows a 300 mm dimension, which is useful but less helpful.

The condition for having a handrail extension beyond the top step is that the wall face continues as in **6.6b**; where it does not, as in **6.6a**, a disabled person climbing the stairs has nothing to pull or push on, and may be unable to get up the top step or the one below it.

Handrails with a circular cross-section and a diameter between 30 and 50 mm are most comfortable to grip. For people who need to grasp a handrail when ascending stairs, the profiles shown in **6.5** range from left to right, with **6.5a** being the most suitable. A handrail as in **6.5d** would not be convenient if its flat top face were wider than 60 mm and there was not a niche to assist grasping.

Handrails to stairs placed as they usually are at about 900 mm above the line of the nosings are convenient for ascending purposes, but not descending, and as previously noted, it is descending which for disabled people and others is more hazardous. Particularly where stairs are steep, it is helpful for there to be a second rail at about 1300 mm, as shown in **6.7**.

Swimming pool access
Vertical ladders of the kind normally used to get in and out of swimming pools can be impossible for disabled people to manage. A suitably planned stepped access is preferable, with handrails that assist both descending and ascending (**6.8**).

Ramps subject to Part M
For Part M purposes a ramp that is less steep than 1:20 is a 'level approach', and not therefore subject to ramp conditions. Among other conditions, a ramp satisfies the M2 requirement (that it is reasonable for disabled people) provided that it is not steeper than 1:15 if individual flights are not longer than 10 m or not steeper than 1:12 if flights are not longer than 5 m; that intermediate landings between flights are not less than 1.2 m long; that it has a raised kerb not less than 100 mm high on any open side; and that it has suitable handrails on each side if its length is more than 2 m.

These conditions, geared to catering for independent wheelchair users, are illustrated in **6.9a** and **b**: to achieve a rise of 633 mm, two ramps with an intermediate landing have a length of 11.5 m, and for a rise of 1333 mm the corresponding length is 21.5 m.

Both with gentle gradients, these ramps ought as a rule to be comfortably manageable by ambulant disabled people, independent wheel-chair users and the pushers of wheelchair users, although the short intermediate landing could cause ambulant disabled people who do not see it to trip and fall. A landing with a length not less than 3 m would be more satisfactory.

Ramps not subject to Part M

The Part M regulation covers new buildings. It does not as a rule apply when existing build-ings are altered to cater for disabled people, involving perhaps the provision of a ramp in place of steps, or a ramp which supplements steps. While there are no rules for the gradi-ent of these ramps, a relatively steep ramp might be in order should there be a stepped approach suitable for ambulant disabled people alongside, whereas it would not be were it the only approach to the building.

Diagrams **6.9c** and **d** show a short ramp with a 1:6 gradient. In **6.9c** a wheelchair user is being pushed up it. With a ramp as steep as this it would be hazardous for a wheelchair user, whether independent or pushed, to go forwards down it, and in **6.9d** the 'pusher' is shown helping the wheelchair user down backwards. As shown in the two diagrams, the ramp has a length of 1500 mm, giving a rise of 250 mm.

It would not be good practice for a ramp as steep as this to serve as the only entrance to a building. Ambulant disabled people, particu-larly for going down purposes, commonly prefer to use suitable steps, and can be disad-vantaged where a ramp is the only option.

While it might be contended that a 1:6 ramp is unacceptable for any wheelchair users, 'wheelchair-accessible' taxis afford an analogy – the portable ramp that is put in place for a wheelchair user to be pushed into or pulled out of a London taxi may, according to circum-stances, have a gradient as steep as 1:4.

Entrances to public buildings

In respect of public buildings a Part M condi-tion is that ramps should have top and bottom landings whose lengths are not less than 1.2 m.

Another, affected by the kerb requirement, is that although their surface widths have to be at least 1.2 m, unobstructed widths can be not less than 1.0 m. Diagrams **6.10a–d**, showing entrances to buildings where the approach to a platform in front of a single-leaf entrance door is by way of a ramp, are considered with regard to these conditions.

Diagram **6.10a** shows a straight approach to the entrance door; it indicates that for a pushed wheelchair user a platform length of 1500 mm is more satisfactory than 1200 mm. Diagram **6.10b** indicates that where the wheel-chair has to be turned to pass through the door a 1200 mm unobstructed ramp width is tight, suggesting that a 1000 mm width would make the manoeuvre extremely difficult. Diagram **6.10c** with an out-opening door shows that the turn would be more easily accomplished with a platform width of 1500 mm. Diagram **6.10d** indicates the space needed where the door is hinged on the side nearer the ramp.

Entrances to Part M housing

For new housing that is subject to the Part M building regulation, the dimensions that come with corresponding design considerations are less than those for public buildings. The unobstructed width of ramps has to be not less than 900 mm, and the width of platforms at the top of ramps has also to be not less than 900 mm.

Diagrams **6.11a–c** are drawn in accord with Part M's minimum design standards. Where the ramp approach is frontal, **6.11a** shows the platform in front of the door having a length of 1200 mm, indicating that a 900 × 900 mm platform would not be satisfactory. Where a turn is involved it cannot be made from a 900 mm wide platform as in **6.11b** and **c**; comparisons here are with **5.36** on page 52 and **6.10b**.

Alterations to entrances to existing buildings

In small high street shops and office buildings it is common for there to be a step to the entrance door, and on occasion two or three steps. When consideration is given to altering such an entrance in order to make it wheelchair-accessible, a satisfactory solution may be found to be impossible. Or if something can be done, the outcome may be that such benefits as there may be for the occasional wheelchair-using customer are outweighed by disadvantages for ambulant users. Associated deficits may be the resultant visual unattractiveness of the premises or the loss of commercially usable floor space.

The matter is illustrated by the examples shown in **6.12–6.17**. All have been drawn from photographs of building entrances where the problem of wheelchair access has been tackled.

In **6.12** an existing step has been replaced by a ramp, a method that is only feasible where the footway outside the shop is sufficiently wide for the ramp not to impede the passage of pedestrians along the footway. In this case the ramp is graded at about 1:7 and there is no platform in front of the door for a wheelchair user to secure himself while opening the door. The outcome is neither convenient for wheelchair users nor ambulant disabled people.

In **6.13** a stepped platform in front of recessed entrance doors has been removed to provide a ramp graded at about 1:9, with there now being no platform in front of the doors for wheelchair users.

In **6.14** the shop's frontage has been altered to accommodate a ramped access with kerbs and railings within the curtilage. The ramp from the street footway to the platform in front of the door is graded at about 1:10, but the side rail is helpful for ambulant disabled people.

In **6.15** the reconstructed approach to the entrance has a ramp on one side and a step on the other, fronted by railings. The ramp gradient is about 1:8 and the step is about 180 mm. Although the outcome does not represent good design, it suits both wheelchair users and ambulant disabled people.

In **6.16** the existing door to a small shop (**6.16a**) had a step about 130 mm high. This was replaced by a new door, which has level access from the adjacent footway (**6.16b**). It opens in over a recessed doormat (**6.16c**),

which, with a short ramp beyond the door swing, is graded at about 1:5 and rises to the floor level of the shop (**6.16d**). For people inside, the drop to the mat by the unguarded kerb could be overlooked.

The entrance to an existing office building is shown in **6.17**. With the entrance door being recessed, the three steps up to the platform in front of the door are associated with a ramp that has been placed within the limited space available; it has a length of about 2.5 m and a gradient of about 1:6.

These six cases are reviewed with regard to the regulatory requirement that when an existing building is altered the access provision made for disabled people is not worse than it was before. Judgements are necessarily subjective in the light of all the circumstances of each case, but the impression is that three of the six (**6.14**, **6.15** and **6.17**) are not worse than they were before, one (**6.13**) is perhaps worse, and two (**6.12** and **6.16**) are worse.

As alterations to existing buildings, these examples illustrate the universal design principle of extending the accommodation parameters of normal provision. More so than for new construction, they demonstrate that for building alterations prescriptive design standards are not in order. The matter is discussed further on page 7 with regard to the provisions of the Disability Discrimination Act.

Passenger lifts
In new public and employment buildings where lifts are provided to satisfy Part M requirements, the advice in the 1999 Part M approved document is that they should have a car whose width is not less than 1100 mm and length not less than 1400 mm, with a door or doors giving an opening width of not less than 800 mm (**6.19**).

In new housing schemes in which a lift gives access to storeys at different levels, the lift will be subject to Part M requirements. The advice in the 1999 Part M Approved Document is that it should be suitable for an unaccompanied wheelchair user; that its car should have a width of not less than 900 mm and a length of not less than 1250 mm, and that its door or doors should give an opening width of not less than 800 mm.

Diagram **6.18** shows that a lift to Part M housing minimum dimensions can accommodate an independent wheelchair user, but is not convenient for the wheelchair user who is being pushed by someone else, as **6.20** indicates.

Referring to BS 2655 standards, an 1100 × 1400 mm lift (**6.20**) is an 8 person general passenger lift, a 1350 × 1400 mm lift (**6.21**) is 10 person, a 1600 × 1400 mm lift is 13 person (**6.22**) and a 1950 × 1400 mm lift is 16 person (**6.23**). Any of these will accommodate a single-pushchair user, a wheelchair user or the user of a small-size scooter (as in **6.21**), but a double-pushchair user needs a door opening wider than 800 mm, for example as in **6.22** or **6.23**.

Stretcher or bed lifts
A lift needs to have an internal length not less than 2400 mm in order to accommodate a stretcher or a bed and an accompanying person.

Through-floor lifts, platform lifts and stairlifts
As noted on page 104, a 2-storey house to Lifetime Homes standard has to be planned to show where a through-floor lift from the ground to first floor could be placed if needed. A through-floor lift designed to accommodate a wheelchair user (not a wheelchair user and a helper) when an existing house is adapted is shown in **6.24**. Suppliers of this and other proprietary lifts illustrated on pages 64 and 65 are listed on page xi.

Shown in **6.25**, a proprietary access lift with retractable steps enables wheelchair users to move between adjoining rooms at different levels whose floors are linked by steps. In **6.25a** the steps are in their normal position. In **6.25b** the steps have been retracted, the barrier is up, and the lift carrying the wheelchair user is beginning to rise. In **6.25c** the lift is raised, the barrier is down and the wheelchair pushes out on the upper floor.

An external vertical wheelchair platform lift is shown in **6.26**, an internal wheelchair platform lift in **6.27**, a stair wheelchair platform lift in **6.28** and a domestic stairlift in **6.29**. For all lifts of these kinds the structural conditions and space parameters needed for their installation are variable according to circumstances. With regard to the advice in the 1999 Part M Approved Document, the provision of wheelchair platform lifts is discussed on page 13.

Escalators
When escalators are planned in public or employment buildings consideration should be given to their specification. When stepping onto an escalator, ambulant disabled people (and others also) need to stabilise themselves before the escalator steps begin to rise. An escalator with three run-on steps (**6.31**) affords more time for this than one with two run-on steps (**6.30**). A note in this connection is that the escalators at London underground stations customarily have five run-on steps.

Refuge spaces
BS 5588 Part 8, the BS code of practice for means of escape for disabled people, advises that a refuge space for disabled people on an escape route from a building should be 1400 × 900 mm. As **6.32** and **6.33** show, this can accommodate a wheelchair user and his or her companion.

Steps and stairs
Commentary page 53

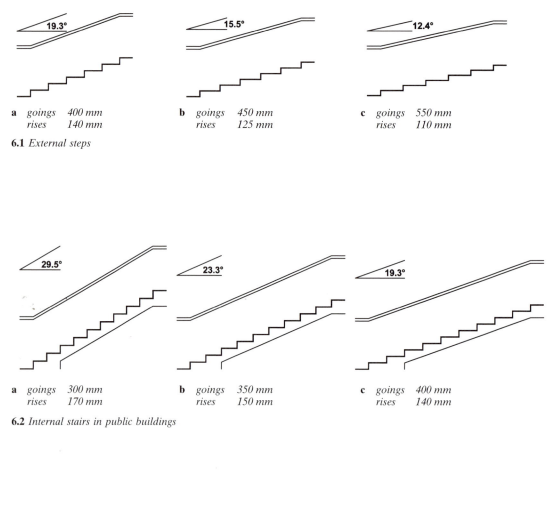

a   *goings*   *400 mm*
     rises   *140 mm*

b   *goings*   *450 mm*
     rises   *125 mm*

c   *goings*   *550 mm*
     rises   *110 mm*

6.1 *External steps*

a   *goings*   *300 mm*
     rises   *170 mm*

b   *goings*   *350 mm*
     rises   *150 mm*

c   *goings*   *400 mm*
     rises   *140 mm*

6.2 *Internal stairs in public buildings*

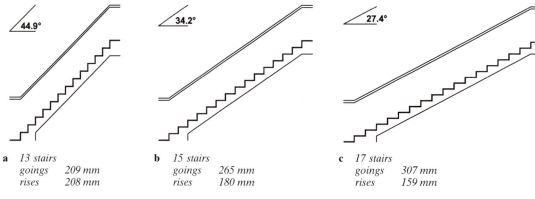

a   *13 stairs*
     goings   *209 mm*
     rises   *208 mm*

b   *15 stairs*
     goings   *265 mm*
     rises   *180 mm*

c   *17 stairs*
     goings   *307 mm*
     rises   *159 mm*

6.3 *Stairs in two-storey housing, floor-to-floor height 2700 mm*

Handrails

Commentary page 54

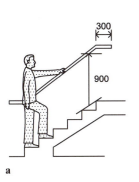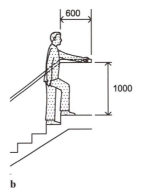

6.4 *Handrails to stairs*

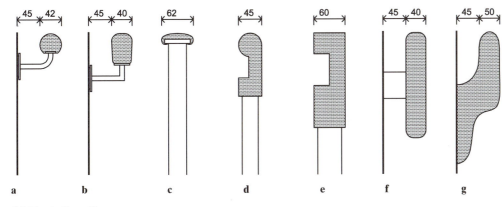

6.5 *Handrail profiles*

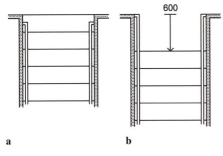

6.6 *Stairway planning, handrail extension*

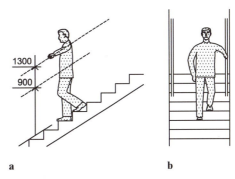

6.7 *Supplementary high-level handrail to steep steps*

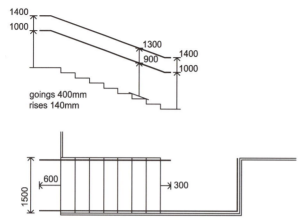

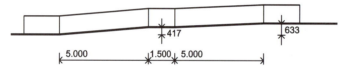

6.8 *Swimming pool stepped access*

Ramps

Commentary page 54

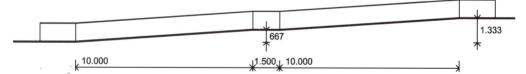

a Ramp in compliance with Part M, 1:12 gradient with handrail and intermediate landing

b Ramp in compliance with Part M, 1:15 gradient with handrail and intermediate landing

c Ramp, 1:6 gradient, wheelchair user being pushed up

d Ramp, 1:6 gradient, wheelchair user being helped down backwards

6.9 *Ramp gradients*

Entrances to buildings

Commentary page 55

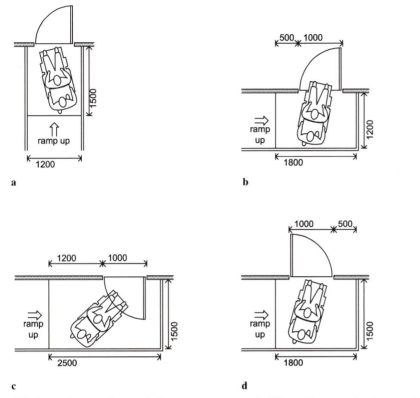

6.10 *Ramped approaches to platforms at entrances to buildings. The examples shown satisfy Part M requirements applicable to new public buildings*

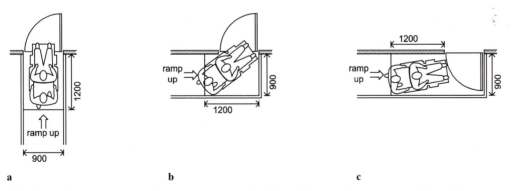

6.11 *Ramped approaches to platforms at entrances to buildings. The examples shown satisfy Part M requirements applicable to new housing*

Alterations to building entrances
Commentary pages 7–9, 55–6

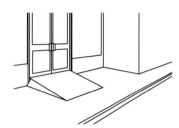

6.12 *Ramp in place of single step at shop entrance*

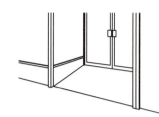

6.13 *Ramp in place of stepped platform at shop entrance*

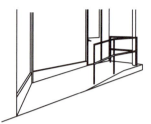

6.14 *Shop frontage altered to provide ramped access*

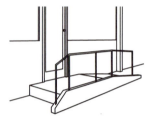

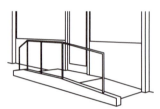

6.15 *Stepped and ramped approach to shop entrance in place of single high step aligned with shop entrance door*

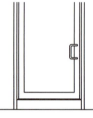

6.16a *Single step aligned with shop entrance door*

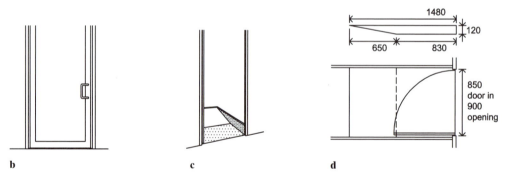

b

c

d

6.16b–d *Shop where existing entrance door as in 6.16a has been replaced by door with level access from pedestrian footway. Recessed doormat inside is ramped beyond door swing to meet shop floor level*

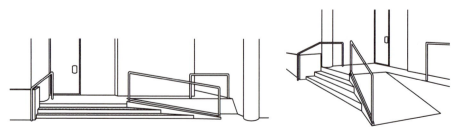

6.17 *Existing building where three steps at entrance have been supplemented by alternative ramped approach*

Lifts
Commentary page 56

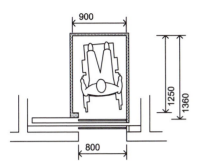

6.18 *Housing, lift to flats as advised to satisfy Part M*

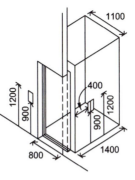

6.19 *Public buildings, lift as advised to satisfy Part M*

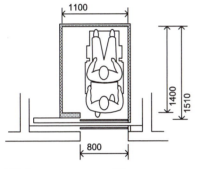

6.20 *8-person passenger lift*

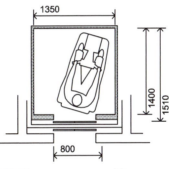

6.21 *10-person passenger lift*

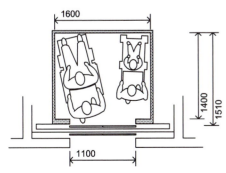

6.22 *13-person passenger lift*

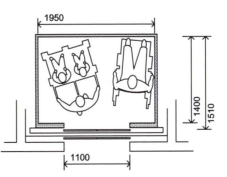

6.23 *16-person passenger lift*

Platform lifts and stairlifts
Commentary page 57

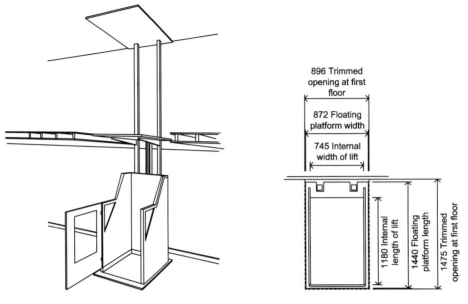

Plan

6.24 *Through-floor lift. Example of provision to be allowed for in planning of Lifetime Homes*

a *Steps in normal position*

b *Steps retracted, barrier up, lift starting to rise*

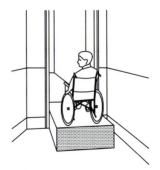

c *Lift raised, barrier down*

6.25 *Retractable access lift*

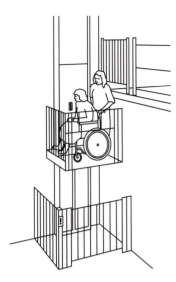

6.26 *External wheelchair platform lift*

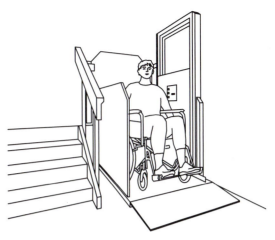

6.27 *Internal wheelchair platform lift*

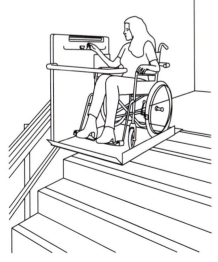

6.28 *Stair wheelchair platform lift*

6.29 *Chair stairlift*

Escalators
Commentary page 57

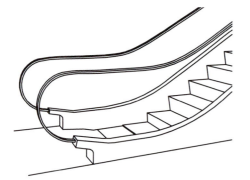

6.30 *Escalator with two run-on steps*

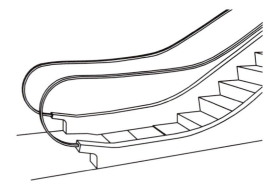

6.31 *Escalator with three run-on steps, affording more space for people unsteady on their feet to stabilise themselves*

Refuge spaces
Commentary page 57

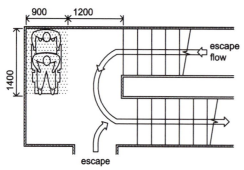

6.32 *Refuge with one wheelchair space*

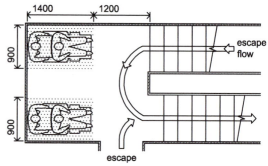

6.33 *Refuge with two wheelchair spaces*

7 Sanitary facilities

The comparison between the bottom-up methodology of universal design and the top-down mode of 'for the disabled' design is demonstrated most markedly in respect of the planning and design of public toilets and wc facilities. Universal design, given its aim to eradicate discrimination by making normal provision suitable for everyone, focuses on normal sanitary facilities and looks at how they can be planned to cater for people with disabilities as well as able-bodied people. By contrast, for-the-disabled design, exemplified in Britain by the edicts of the Part M building regulation, starts by assuming that disabled people are not normal people and that to meet their special needs special provision ought to be made for them. An effect of this, manifested in the Part M approved document, is the proposition that in public buildings the needs of all disabled people can be accommodated by prescribing a special for-the-disabled unisex toilet which when provided will make it unnecessary for normal toilet facilities to be accessible to disabled people. Special provision is thus added on to what in an uncontrolled fashion is done for normal people, the effects on both sides being discriminatory.

Public toilets – discrimination against women

Universal design is the key to tackling architectural discrimination, and where the issue is sanitary facilities, in particular wcs in public toilet facilities, it is women who are most vulnerable to discrimination. There is a range of reasons why architectural discrimination against women is endemic, one being that architects tend not to think when they plan toilet facilities in public buildings. Their common practice is to map out two approximately equal areas of space on plan drawings, allocating one to men and the other to women. Urinals occupy much less space than wc compartments, the effect when the areas are filled being more amenities for men than there are for women.

In public buildings around Britain the number of urinals and wcs that men are given in public toilet facilities is typically twice as many as the wcs that women get – examples are cited in Chapter 1 on page 6. The effect in terms of discrimination – or being 'disabled' on account of not being able to use the facilities – is that women are four times more vulnerable than men. This is because, along with being given only half as many toilet facilities, there is the time factor – women take longer than men when using them, relevant research indicating that on average they take twice as long.

To achieve parity where the incidence of usage is roughly the same, women should have twice as many amenities; in practice what this means when cloakrooms are planned is that women ought to get about three times as much space as men.

Comparative plan arrangements

Diagram **7.1** illustrates the issue. With a unisex toilet for disabled people being placed elsewhere, they show what may happen when public toilet facilities are planned which give women the same amount of space as men, twice as much and three times as much. To inform comparisons, the provision shown for men is identical in all three; its dimensions are 3.0 m on the x axis and 5.5 m on the y, giving an overall area which permits the placing of eight toilet amenities – two wc compartments and six urinals.

In **7.1a** the women's area is within the same dimensions. Compared with the men's eight amenities, women with their wc compartments have five – not 16, as there would be were there no discrimination in favour of men. In **7.1b** the dimension on the x axis of the women's side is 6.0 m, giving a plan arrangement that permits the placing of ten wc compartments, still short of the ideal 16. In **7.1c** parity is obtained; the overall plan arrangement, with its 75/25 space distribution, permits the placing of 16 wc compartments on the women's side.

With regard to the planning of public toilet facilities, the three diagrams were purposely drafted to illustrate space distribution, and the disposition of the facilities within the areas shown ought not to be viewed as representing good practice. Had that been intended, the proportion of overall space given to women in the **7.1c** parity diagram could have been relatively greater. A series of reasons for this are noted for this.

The size of normal wc compartments
The wc compartments shown on the plans, while being of a kind that could be found in many recently designed public toilet areas, are uncomfortably small for both men and women to use, given their in-opening doors and plan dimensions of the order of 1500 × 850 mm. Had more convenient and spacious wc compartments for all users been shown, the proportion of space occupied by them on the plans would have been greater, the effect, with more of them being on the women's side, being to increase the overall amount of space given to women.

The customary practice when public toilets are planned is for the wc compartments for women to be identical in size to those for men. But for three reasons women are more commonly disadvantaged than men by the

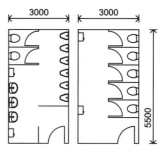

a *Area ratio 1:1. Males 8 toilet facilities (6 urinals + 2 wcs); females 5 (5 wcs)*

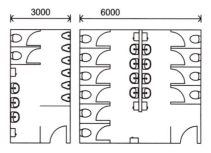

b *Area ratio 1:2. Males 8, females 10*

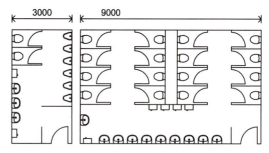

c *Area ratio 1:3. Males 8, females 16*

7.1 *Public cloakrooms, distribution of male/female toilet facilities*

7.2 *Wc with close-coupled cistern*

7.3 *Wc with external cistern*

constricted size and awkward configuration of a typical wc compartment in a public lavatory. The first is that the clothes they wear are more prone to sweeping the wc seat and hence to contamination. The second is that they always have to sit down or squat, which involves the adjustment of clothing (and sometimes taking off an overcoat) in a confined space. The third is that a sanitary waste disposal bin placed to one side of the wc restricts the manoeuvring space available.

Powder room facilities
Relative space for women will also be increased in cloakrooms where there are powder room facilities, meaning that, as well as wash basins, there is an area with mirrors and other amenities where women can groom themselves.

Wc facilities, general provision

In different contexts wcs are shown on the series of plan diagrams from **7.1** through to **7.79**. Some depict a close-coupled cistern, as is customary in domestic housing and small buildings. Others do not, the understanding there being that the cistern supplying them is external, as happens where there is ducting behind a row of wcs. In the context of universal design, the difference on plan between the two can be significant. With a close-coupled cistern (**7.2**), the front edge of the wc bowl usually projects about 740 mm from the rear wall, whereas with an external cistern (**7.3**) the projection is usually about 550 mm.

Normal wc compartments
The comparison is shown by **7.11** and **7.12**, both of which have internal dimensions 800 × 1500 mm. Neither is at all convenient for a mother with a small child, but where the cistern is external (**7.11**) there is considerably more space for manoeuvre than when it is coupled to the wc (**7.12**).

With the same width, **7.13** and **7.14** illustrate the benefits of an 1800 depth dimension in

place of 1500 mm. With an external cistern (**7.13**) it is practicable (although space is tight) for the mother to bring a child in a pushchair into the wc compartment with her. With a coupled cistern (**7.14**) that would not be manageable, although there is adequate space for the mother to bring the child in without the pushchair and close the door.

Out-opening doors
The **7.11–14** plans are not shown with an out-opening door. For all four, it is however apparent that mother, child and pushchair management would be facilitated if the door were to open out; **7.17** and **7.32** are relevant.

Wc compartments with wash basins
Diagrams **7.15a** and **b** show 1200 mm wide wc compartments with a corner wash basin. These give convenient space for a mother and child, with the 1800 mm depth of **7.15b** giving room for pushchair manoeuvre.

A related issue here is hygiene. For health reasons it is desirable that there is always a hand wash basin alongside a wc. But in public cloakrooms the established custom in Britain, both on men's and women's sides, is that wc compartments have only a wc, with wash basins being located elsewhere. Relevant research findings have shown that men when they have used urinals tend not to bother to wash their hands, whereas women do when they have used wcs. Relatedly, women consider it more desirable that as a matter of course there ought to be a wash basin within any wc compartment[1].

Sanitary bins
In public toilets in Britain, the near-universal custom is for sanitary bins to be placed in women's wc compartments. As **7.16** shows, they can severely restrict the ability of a woman to manage comfortably within the wc compartment, particularly where the width is only 800 mm, as in **7.16a**. Where the width is 900 mm or more, management can be easier if the centre line of the wc is offset, as shown in **7.16c** and **7.16d**.

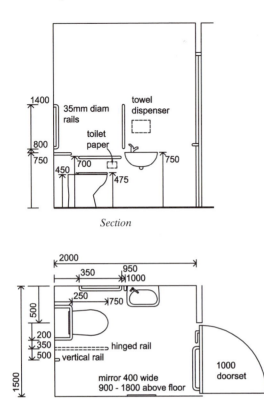

Section

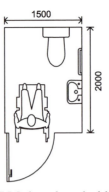

7.5 *Independent wheelchair user entering through out-opening door*

Plan

7.4 *The Part M unisex toilet*

The potential scope of normal wc facilities
The analysis of **7.11–7.16** has indicated that normal wc facilities can when suitably planned conveniently accommodate a broad range of building users beyond the normal able-bodied people in levels 1 and 2 of the universal design pyramid (**1.1** on page 3). The women in level 3 of the pyramid are catered for if regard is had to avoiding discrimination with wc provision being on the lines of **7.1c**. Where there is level access to toilet facilities, most of those in levels 4 and 5 can be conveniently accommodated. Those who could still be left out will in the main be the wheelchair users in levels 6, 7 and 8. Universal design has answers for them, but before commenting on relevant diagrams later in the chapter, the effects of taking the 'for the disabled' top-down route set by Part M are examined.

Part M unisex toilet

The 1999 Part M Approved Document presents design guidance for two 'for-the-disabled' wc compartments. One is a wheelchair wc compartment (**7.4**), referred to in this book as the Part M unisex toilet. The other is a wc compartment for ambulant disabled people (**7.17**).

In a new public building the rule is that there must be at least one Part M unisex toilet. It may be in a location set apart from normal toilet facilities, and in practice it may be one that is kept locked, meaning that those disabled people who do not have with them the special key to unlock its door may be prevented from using it. An associated condition is that a wc compartment designed for ambulant disabled people should be provided within each range of wc compartments included in storeys which are not designed to be accessible to wheelchair users, meaning areas that can only be reached by a stairway.

The ambulant disabled wc compartment has to be equipped with grab rails. These may be helpful for some, but among ambulant disabled people generally the critical need is for public toilets to be reachable without having to use stairs[2].

The plan layout, design and equipment of the Part M unisex toilet are the same as for the BS5810 toilet presented by the British Standards Institution in 1979, for which the

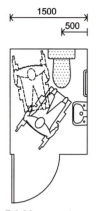

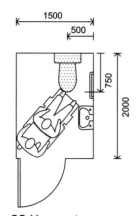

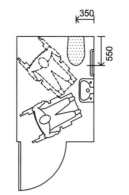

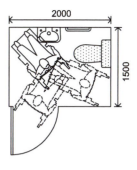

7.6 *Manoeuvring space, independent wheelchair user*

7.7 *Manoeuvring space, pushed wheelchair user*

7.8 *Manoeuvring space, we rearranged*

7.9 *Manoeuvring space, plan arrangement turned*

research programme was undertaken during the years 1972 to 1974.

Given the variability of the characteristics and capabilities of wheelchair users and other disabled people, it was never realistic to suppose that all would be suited by it, as has been confirmed by messages from disabled people reported in the disability media, journal articles, and by the findings of the Department of the Environment's 1990 research project, *Sanitary provision for people with special needs*.

The plan arrangement
The Part M toilet with its 2000 × 1500 mm plan dimensions has an out-opening door – an in-opening door could have made it impossible for a wheelchair user to get in and close the door behind him. An effect of the space layout is, however, that an independent wheelchair user when entering cannot readily reach back and close the door (**7.5**). And with the wc in a corner off the far back side, an unavoidable consequence of the plan arrangement is that the space for wheelchair manoeuvre is inefficiently distributed; it is difficult, if not impossible, for a wheelchair to be turned around inside (**7.6, 7.7**).

The 500 mm dimension from the centre line of the wc to the side wall (**7.6**) was set so that an attendant helping a wheelchair user to

transfer might place himself or herself in the back corner. A demerit of this is that the important side horizontal rail is too far from the wc to be convenient for pushing-up purposes; as is shown in **7.18**, the preferred dimension is about 350 mm.

The 750 mm dimension from the rear wall to the face of the wc (**7.4, 7.7**) was prescribed to allow a wheelchair user to place himself or herself parallel to the wc in order to facilitate transfer; given the large main wheels at the rear, that could only be done by projecting the wc forwards.

In practice it has been found that the small advantage was outweighed by the penalties; aside from the construction problems, an effect was to reduce vital wheelchair manoeuvring space within the compartment. As **7.8** shows by comparison with **7.6** and **7.7**, a rearrangement of the position and projection of the wc would give appreciably more space for wheelchair turning.

As already noted, the space for wheelchair manoeuvre is inefficiently distributed where a Part M unisex toilet is arranged as shown in the Approved Document. Advantageously and without altering the overall dimensions, the layout would be turned on its side as in **7.9**, the effect being to give much more convenient wheelchair manoeuvring space and making it easier for the door to be closed or opened.

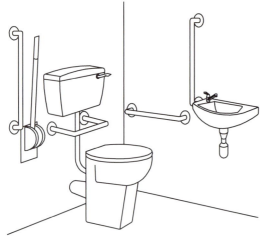

7.10 *Grab rails for Part M unisex toilet*

Table 7.1 Part M toilet: grab rails used by people in samples of wheelchair users

	Public buildings (%)	Employment buildings (%)
Side horizontal rail on wall by wc	64	56
Drop-down rail on open side of wc	36	15
Vertical rail on side wall by wc	21	14
Low horizontal rail behind wc	14	14
Vertical rail on rear wall on open side of wc	8	12
None	14	29
Don't know/not stated	4	2

Source: *Designing for the Disabled – The New Paradigm* p. 377

Transfers to and from the wc

To assist wheelchair users and other disabled people to transfer to and from the wc, the Part M unisex toilet comes with five grab rails (**7.10**). For the Department of the Environment's sanitary provision research project, questions about their usefulness were put to people in the samples of wheelchair users who said they had used a Part M-type toilet, 132 in respect of toilets in public buildings, and 84 for ones in employment buildings. Table 7.1 lists the percentages who had used each of the five.

Wc compartments for ambulant disabled people as advised in the Part M Approved Document have horizontal and vertical rails to each side of the wc (**7.17**). As indicated in Table 7.1, the side rails are the more helpful.

The position of the horizontal side rail

For the person who raises himself from the wc seat to a standing position by pushing on the horizontal side rail, the closer the rail is to the wc the more convenient it is (**7.18**). A 300 mm dimension from the centre line of the wc to the side wall (**7.18c**) is more convenient than 400 mm (**7.18b**), and 400 mm is better than the unsatisfactory 500 mm Part M arrangement (**7.18a**).

Where the dimension to the side wall is more than 400 mm, a drop-down side rail of the kind shown in **7.19a** may be preferred. With an external cistern a 250 mm dimension from the centre line of the wc to the line of the rail is suitable (**7.19b**), and 300 mm with a close-coupled cistern where the cistern affects the rail's fixing points (**7.19c**).

Transfers from a wheelchair

Diagrams **7.20–7.31** show ways by which transfers from a wheelchair to a wc seat may be effected; they are not exhaustive and assume, which is not always the case, that reverse transfers are likewise. Other than in **7.22** and **7.24** the wheelchair is shown with the footrests folded back, and in most of the positions shown an armrest will be removed. In diagrams where the wheelchair user is being assisted the helpers are shown tinted. The dimensions shown are scaled off the drawings and do not indicate preferred utilisation spaces.

In **7.20** the wheelchair user is able to lift himself from the chair seat, stand, turn and lower himself onto the wc.

In **7.21** the wheelchair user is not able to put weight on his feet but with strong arms can lift himself to transfer from wheelchair to wc seat.

In **7.22** the wheelchair user pushes through the back of the chair, which has a zip for opening the canvas of the backrest, and slides onto the wc seat.

Diagrams **7.23–5** show side transfers from wheelchair to wc seat. In **7.23** and **7.25** the wheelchair user puts some weight on his feet; in **7.24** he does not do so. For the **7.24** and **7.25** moves a side rail as in **7.23** would help; with it a **7.24**-type transfer by a wheelchair user unable to put any weight on his feet could be made with the wheelchair aligned as in **7.25**.

In **7.26** the wheelchair user stands to transfer; the difference between this and **7.20** is that the wheelchair user needs a fixed side rail in order to effect the transfer.

In **7.27–9** the wheelchair user is assisted by a helper. In **7.27** the helper lifts the wheelchair user bodily from wheelchair to wc. In **7.28** and **7.29** the wheelchair user is helped to raise himself to a standing position and is then helped to turn in order to transfer onto the wc.

In **7.30** and **31** the wheelchair user is assisted by two helpers, with the plan layout giving clear space to either side of the wc, as for example shown in **7.52**. In **7.30** the wheelchair user can stand and turn when he has been lifted to his feet. In **7.31** the wheelchair user cannot put any weight on his feet and has to be lifted bodily for the move to the wc.

Lateral transfer options
In a public building the Part M unisex toilet usually comes singly; a consequence being that there is allowance for lateral wheelchair transfer from one side only. Most wheelchair users when using a wc do not, however, transfer laterally – of those who were interviewed for the sanitary provision research project, about one in four said that they did, and of these a further one in four were not able to transfer to both left and right. These findings suggest that some 8 per cent of all wheelchair users who take their wheelchair into public toilets could be unable to transfer to the wc owing to one-way-only lateral transfer provision. The alternative to the transfer-one-side-only Part

M-type unisex toilet is a peninsular layout of the kind shown in **7.52**.

Wc facilities with limited wheelchair access

For comparison with the Part M unisex plan, the diagrams on page 80 show wc facilities which give restricted wheelchair access.

Diagram **7.32** has the same internal dimensions as the normal wc compartment shown in **7.14**, but with an out-opening door and external cistern permits restricted wheelchair access, making it suitable for a wheelchair user who can stand to transfer or who uses the wc as a urinal.

Diagrams **7.33–9** show wc facilities with a wash basin. With a 1000 mm out-opening door, **7.33** and **7.34** have the same internal dimensions as **7.15a**, and so does **7.36** where the layout is turned. In these examples space for wheelchair access is tight, though easier with the **7.36** than the **7.33** or **7.35** layout. In **7.35** the wc is closer to the side wall than in **7.33**, making wheelchair access slightly easier.

Relately with a 1000 mm out-opening door, **7.34** and **7.38** have the same internal dimensions as **7.15b**, as also does **7.39** where the layout is turned. In these examples there is space for wheelchair access. As **7.38** and **7.39** show by comparison with **7.35** and **7.36**, a double-pushchair user needs more space inside a wc compartment than an independent wheelchair user.

Diagram **7.37** shows how a wc compartment to the same internal dimensions as the Part M unisex toilet can give wheelchair access where it has an in-opening door. In this case a 900 mm door is shown; with a 1000 mm door the door would be less easy to close with the wheelchair user inside.

Diagrams **7.38** and **7.39** have a 1000 m doorset giving an opening of not less than 875 mm. They show that a double-pushchair user needs more space inside a wc compartment than an independent wheelchair user; the comparison is with **7.35** and **7.36**.

Part M housing, accessible wcs

In 1999 the Part M building regulation was extended to cover new housing. Plan diagrams in the Approved Document showed how 'accessible' wc compartments should be approached either frontally or obliquely, and these are illustrated in **7.40** and **7.41**.

Related advice is that the wc compartment door opens outward in accord with prescribed dimensions (those set out in Table 5.1 on page 43); that the wc compartment provides a clear space for wheelchair users to access the wc and the wash basin is positioned so that it does not impede access; that to enable transfer the wheelchair should be able to approach within 400 mm of the front of the wc; and that 500 mm dimensions either side of the wc centre line are preferred to the 450 minimum.

Diagrams **7.42–5** show examples of how in practice the advice has been interpreted in social housing schemes designed by PRP Architects.

Wc facilities with wheelchair-accessible provision

As for example shown by **7.34** and **7.36**, there are independent wheelchair users who can manage without undue difficulty in wc compartments which are considerably less spacious than the authorised Part M unisex toilet with its 2000 × 1500 mm dimensions. And as this commentary has indicated, the approved Part M layout (**7.4**) has deficits, the principal one being that the clear space internally is insufficient to turn a wheelchair around or do so without difficulty.

2000 × 1500 mm alternatives

Of the 2000 × 1500 mm plan diagrams so far examined, the most satisfactory for wheelchair users generally is **7.9**. A variant of it with more clear space for manoeuvring – though with a basin that is less easy to reach from the wc – is shown in **7.46**.

Diagram **7.47** shows the effect of substituting a drop-down rail as in **7.19a** for the fixed side rail (**7.18a**) that does not satisfactorily serve its purpose. This serves for an assistant to help from the corner at the back of the wc but wheelchair turning space is restricted.

2200 × 1700 mm

To give comfortable space for wheelchair turning, particularly where the turning has to be done by the wheelchair user's attendant, the Part M toilet 2000 and 1500 mm dimensions need to be increased. In **7.48** and **7.49** they are 2200 and 1700 mm, an advantage of which is that the door can open in, making it easier for either the wheelchair user or helper to open and close it.

Peninsular layouts

The Part M 'L' layout, i.e. with the wc in a corner position, does not suit all wheelchair users and their helpers. Those wheelchair users who are most severely handicapped, in particular those who need two helpers to assist them onto and off the wc, commonly prefer a peninsular layout, one where the wc is freestanding, as in **7.52**. An advantage is that it caters for those wheelchair users who transfer laterally, but can do so in one direction only and need to have the wc on a particular side, either to their left or the right.

A peninsular layout would not suit all other disabled people, the findings of the DOE sanitary provision project indicating that the majority of wheelchair users prefer the L layout, subject to the 2000 and 1500 mm dimensions being increased.

As shown in **7.50**, it is practicable to have a freestanding wc within a 2000 × 1500 mm plan layout. But manoeuvring space is restricted, and there is insufficient space to turn a wheelchair around. With increased overall dimensions, 2500 × 1700 in **7.51** and 2500 × 2000 in **7.52**, the door can open in. An unavoidable feature of a peninsular layout is that the wash basin cannot be reached from the wc.

The low rail behind the wc

To meet Part M requirements, a low horizontal rail is advised behind the wc (**7.10**). As shown in **7.53**, it cannot be fixed where the cistern is close-coupled, and where that is not the case as in **7.54**, care needs to be taken that the wc seat when lifted does not fall forward.

Lobbies to unisex toilets and cloakrooms

The lobbies to unisex toilets shown in **7.55–8** do not have as much space for wheelchair manoeuvre as would be desirable. Diagrams **7.55** and **7.56** show lobbies with a configuration similar to that advised in the 1999 Part M Approved Document and shown in **7.63a** and **7.62a**. With lobbies that have the same internal dimensions, **7.56** shows that movement in and out is easier where the entrance door opens out rather than in (**7.55**). Where both doors open in, wheelchair manoeuvre is more manageable where the lobby has a depth of the order of 3000 mm as indicated in **7.62b** or is planned as in **7.63b**.

Diagram **7.57** shows a lobby arrangement where a Part M-type wc compartment is turned on its side. A similar arrangement is shown in **7.58** where a 2200 × 1700 mm wc compartment has an in-opening door, as in **7.49**.

The **7.59** diagrams show screened cloakroom lobbies without doors. Wider openings and lobby spaces are needed by pushed wheelchair users and double-pushchair users (**7.59b**) than by independent wheelchair users (**7.59a**), with scooter users requiring substantially more space (**7.59c**).

Related comparisons are shown in **7.60a** and **b** where lobbies have an entrance door and screened internal opening.

In **7.61–4** the Part M advice for the planning of internal lobbies is shown in the **a** examples of enclosed cloakroom lobbies which have 900 mm doors. Corresponding layouts that are more spacious and have 1000 mm doors are shown in the **b** examples.

Wash basins

For all users, a demerit of a wash basin with a typical sculptured configuration (**7.65**) is that it gives virtually no space for the placement of washing, shaving and grooming equipment. A wide basin as in **7.66** serves better, or an inset basin in a desk shelf as in **7.67**.

The impracticability of placing a single basin at a height that suits all users is demonstrated in **4.11** on page 37; where there is a row of basins one or more may be at a different height from others. With the wheelchair user approaching an end basin from the side, **7.68** shows that hand and face washing is less comfortable where basin centres are at 650 mm than 750 mm (**7.69**) or wider.

Baths and bathrooms

Reflecting the need there is with low-cost housing in Britain to economise on space in bathrooms in order to maximise space in living rooms and bedrooms, **7.70** and **7.72** show examples of bathrooms in social housing designed by PRP Architects. The **7.70** layout allows an independent wheelchair user to get past the in-opening door with some difficulty, but there is space for manoeuvre where the door opens out as in **7.71**. In **7.72** the wheelchair user cannot get in and close the door, but where it opens out (**7.73**) he or she can.

Diagrams **7.74** and **7.75** show more spacious bathroom plans in social housing designed by PRP Architects to suit wheelchair users. In both, the platform at the head end of the bath allows the wheelchair user who can do so to transfer laterally in order to get into the bath, or wash in a seated position.

In a bathroom which has a hand-held shower associated with the bath but where there is no space for a platform at the head end of the bath, a portable bench seat (**7.77**) with suitable grab rails on the side wall may enable a wheelchair user to use the shower. Relatedly, this can benefit many ambulant disabled people.

In **7.74**, as in **7.73**, the position of the wc means that a wheelchair user cannot easily reach the bath taps. For wheelchair users and other disabled people, it can be helpful if there is ducting or a platform at the foot end of the bath (**7.76**).

Where a bathroom has a shower cubicle as well as or in place of a bath, a cubicle with a tip-up bench seat as shown in **7.82** may suit wheelchair users or other disabled people.

Shower rooms

Diagrams **7.78** and **7.79** show examples of wc/shower rooms on the ground floor of social housing designed by PRP Architects. In both, the understanding is that the shower area has a floor that allows a wheelchair user to drive over it. For this, a proprietary product such as the Neatdek level access shower grille (**7.80**) may be suitable.

For showering in a shower area a wheelchair user may transfer to a shower chair such as that shown in **2.8**. A person seated on a shower chair in shower compartments with standard-size Neatdek grilles is shown in **7.81a** and **b**.

The shower compartment with a tip-up bench seat shown in **7.82** is in accord with the shower compartment advised in the 1999 Part M Approved Document for meeting Part M requirements.

Dressing cubicles

The dressing cubicle shown in **7.83** is in accord with that advised in the 1999 Part M approved document for meeting Part M requirements.

Urinals

The urinals at 600 mm centres shown in **7.84** afford less room for convenient management than those in **7.85** with 700 mm centres.

Notes on the height of urinals are on page 32, diagrams on page 36.

Wc facilities: general provision
Commentary page 69

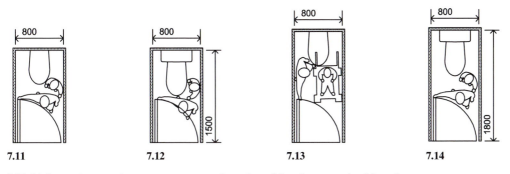

7.11 **7.12** **7.13** **7.14**

7.11–14 *Spaces in normal wc compartments as in male and female zones of public toilets*

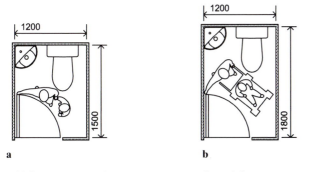

a **b**

7.15 *Spaces in normal wc compartments with wash basins*

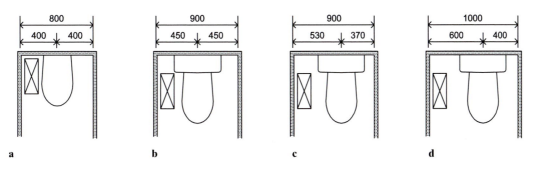

a **b** **c** **d**

7.16 *Sanitary bins for women. The example shown has a width of 150 mm, a length of 380 mm and a height of 510 mm*

Transfers to and from wc

Commentary page 72

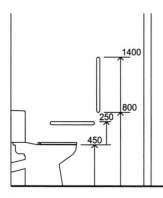

Section

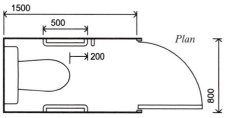

Plan

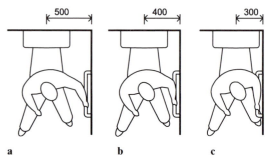

a   b   c

7.17 *Grab rails in wc compartment for ambulant disabled people, as advised in 1999 Part M Approved Document*

7.18 *Placing of the horizontal side rail with regard to the user's ease of rising to a standing position*

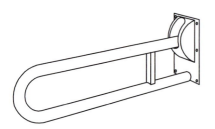

7.19a *Drop-down side rail*

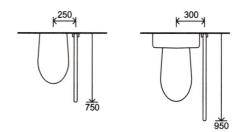

7.19b *Drop-down side rail to wc with external cistern*

7.19c *Drop-down side rail to wc with close-coupled cistern*

Wheelchair users, transfers to and from wc

Commentary page 72

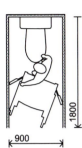

7.20 *Unaided standing transfer*

900 / 1800

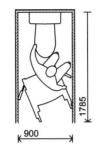

7.21 *Unaided seat-to-seat frontal transfer*

900 / 1785

7.22 *Unaided seat-to-seat transfer through back of chair*

900 / 1540

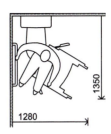

7.23 *Unaided seat-to-seat oblique transfer*

1280 / 1350

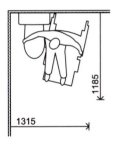

7.24 *Unaided seat-to-seat transfer*

1315 / 1185

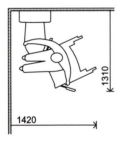

7.25 *Unaided seat-to-seat transfer*

1420 / 1310

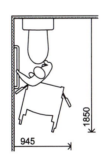

7.26 *Unaided standing transfer*

945 / 1850

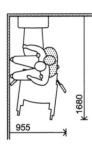

7.27 *Assisted seat-to-seat transfer*

955 / 1680

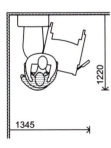

7.28 *Assisted standing transfer*

1345 / 1220

7.29 *Assisted standing transfer*

1010 / 1390

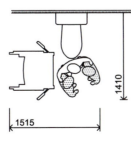

7.30 *Assisted standing transfer with two helpers*

1515 / 1410

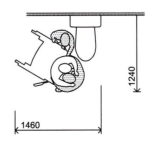

7.31 *Assisted seat-to-seat transfer with two helpers*

1460 / 1240

Wc facilities: limited wheelchair access

Commentary page 73

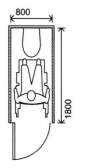

7.32 *Wc compartment with 800 mm out-opening door*

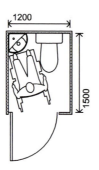

7.33 *Wc compartment with 1000 mm out-opening door*

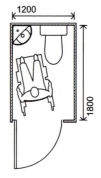

7.34 *Wc compartment with 1000 mm out-opening door*

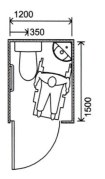

7.35 *Wc compartment with 1000 mm out-opening door*

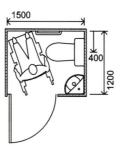

7.36 *Wc compartment with 1000 mm out-opening door*

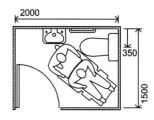

7.37 *Wc compartment with 900 mm in-opening door, to same internal dimensions as Part M unisex toilet*

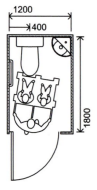

7.38 *Wc compartment with 1000 mm out-opening door, showing access for double-pushchair user*

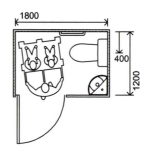

7.39 *Wc compartment with 1000 mm out-opening door, showing access for double-pushchair user*

Part M housing, accessible wcs
Commentary page 74

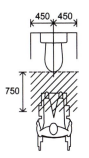

7.40 *Part M Approved Document advice, clear space for frontal access to wc*

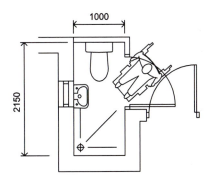

7.41 *Part M Approved Document advice, clear space for oblique access to wc*

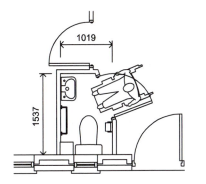

7.42 *Accessible wc, as in house plan 9.4, p 107*

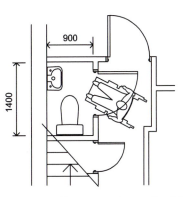

7.43 *Accessible wc, as in house plan 9.5, p 107*

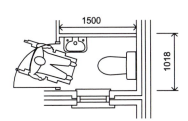

7.44 *Accessible wc, as in house plan 9.6, p 108*

7.45 *Accessible wc, with shower as in comparable house plan 9.8, p 109*

Wc facilities: wheelchair-accessible provision

Commentary pages 74–5

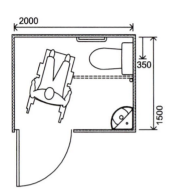

7.46 Variant of Part M unisex toilet with 1000 mm out-opening door on longer side wall, and corner basin

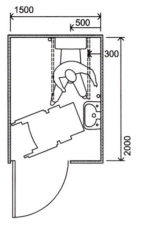

7.47 Part M unisex toilet with drop-down side rail to both sides of wc

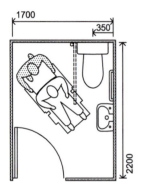

7.48 Larger size variant of Part M unisex toilet with 900 mm in opening-door

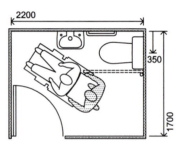

7.49 Larger size variant of Part M unisex toilet with 900 mm in opening-door on longer side wall

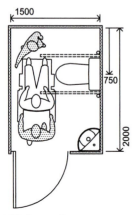

7.50 Peninsular wc in same space as Part M unisex toilet

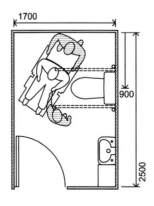

7.51 Peninsular wc with 900 mm in-opening door

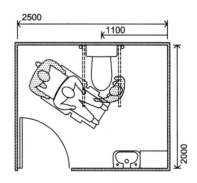

7.52 Peninsular wc with 900 mm in-opening door

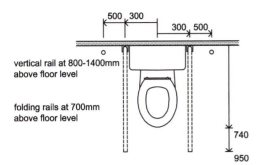

vertical rail at 800-1400mm
above floor level

folding rails at 700mm
above floor level

7.53 *Position of folding rails where cistern is close-coupled*

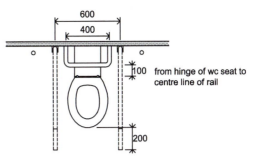

100 from hinge of wc seat to
centre line of rail

200

7.54 *Position of folding rails fixed behind wc where cistern is not close-coupled. Rail is at 250 mm above face of wc bowl*

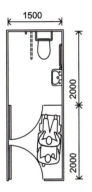

7.55 *Lobby to Part M unisex toilet*

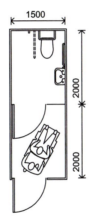

7.56 *Lobby to Part M unisex toilet*

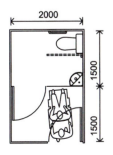

7.57 *Lobby to variant of Part M unisex toilet*

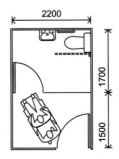

7.58 *Lobby to large size unisex toilet*

Cloakroom lobbies
Commentary page 75

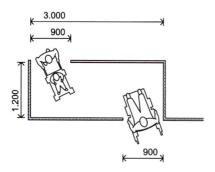

a *Single-pushchair user and independent wheelchair user*

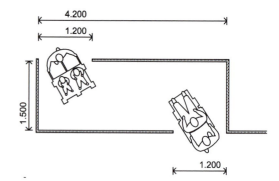

b *Double-pushchair user and pushed wheelchair user*

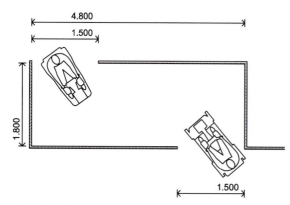

c *3- and 4-wheel electric scooter users*

7.59 *Lobbies with open access to cloakrooms*

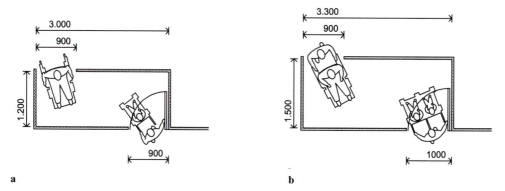

a

b

7.60 *Entrance door and internal clear opening to cloakrooms*

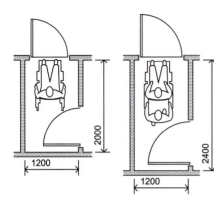

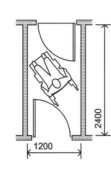

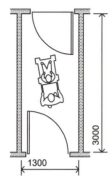

7.61a *Part M example*   **7.61b** *Corresponding example*   **7.62a** *Part M example*   **7.62b** *Corresponding example*

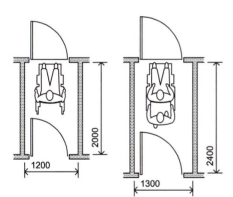

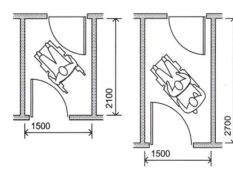

7.63a *Part M example*   **7.63b** *Corresponding example*   **7.64a** *Part M example*   **7.64b** *Corresponding example*

7.61–4 *Enclosed cloakroom lobbies*

Wash basins

Commentary page 75

7.65 *Typical wash basin*

7.66 *Wide basin*

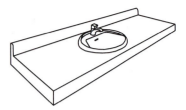

7.67 *Basin in desk shelf*

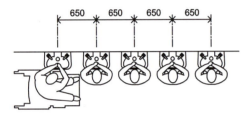

7.68 *Wash basins, 650 mm centres*

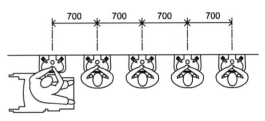

7.69 *Wash basins, 750 mm centres*

Baths and bathrooms

Commentary page 75

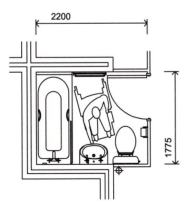

7.70 *Bathroom in social housing scheme*

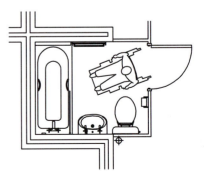

7.71 *Bathroom, as 7.70 with out-opening door*

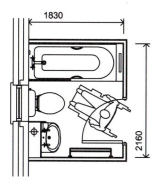

7.72 *Bathroom in social housing scheme*

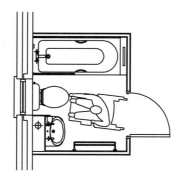

7.73 *Bathroom, as 7.72 with out-opening door*

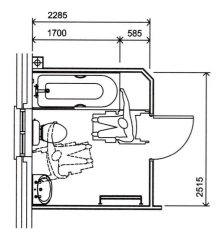

7.74 *Bathroom in social housing for wheelchair users*

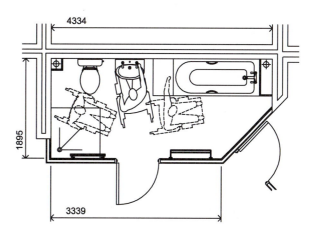

7.75 *Bathroom in social housing for wheelchair users*

7.76 *Wheelchair user reaching towards bath taps*

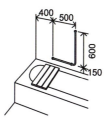

7.77 *Bath seat*

Shower rooms
Commentary page 76

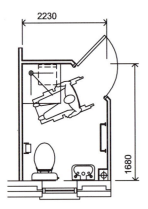

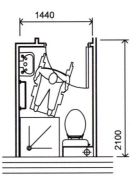

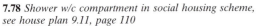

7.78 *Shower w/c compartment in social housing scheme, see house plan 9.11, page 110*

7.79 *Shower w/c compartment in social housing scheme where shower area is level with floor*

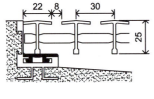

7.80 *Level access shower grille*

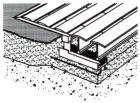

a

b

7.81 *Plans of level access shower as shown in 7.80. The figure represents a wheelchair user in a shower chair as in* **2.8**, *page 20*

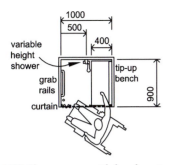

7.82 *Shower room with bench seat*

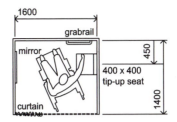

7.83 *Dressing cubicle*

Urinals

Commentary page 76

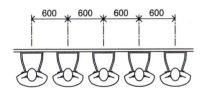

7.84 *Bowl urinals at 600 mm centres*

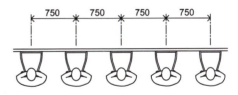

7.85 *Bowl urinals at 750 mm centres*

8 Tiered seating, hotel guestrooms, car parking

Tiered seating and wheelchair spaces

To satisfy the M4 requirement of the Building Regulations, that reasonable provision is made to accommodate disabled people in a building which contains audience or spectator seating, the 1999 Part M Approved Document presents guidance regarding provision for wheelchair users in theatres, cinemas, concert halls, sports stadia, etc.

Of the total of fixed audience or spectator seats available to the public, the Part M rule is that 6 or 1/100th, whichever is the greater, should be 'wheelchair spaces'. With a width not less than 900 mm and a depth not less than 1400 mm, these spaces should be kept clear or readily provided by removing seats; they should give a clear view of the event, and they should be dispersed so that wheelchair users can sit next to able-bodied or disabled companions.

With regard to the implementation of this advice, **8.1–3** show tiered seating and wheelchair spaces, and **8.4** the plan and section of the cinema at the Arc in Stockton-on-Tees. The Arc, opened in 1999, is a theatre and cultural complex designed by RHWL Architects. The six wheelchair spaces that the cinema with its 125 seats needed to have are in locations where fixed seats can be removed.

Whether fixed seating is all at the same level, is on tiers which are gently raked as in **8.4b**, or in tiers which are steeply raked as in **8.1**, the same design problem is posed where wheelchair users are to be in spaces placed in front of other spectators.

The problem is examined by looking first at **8.1**. The y dimension is the same for each tier

and so is the x front-to-back dimension. The four heads in the centre rows represent adult people of average height, and, with head height and eye level for each being the same, each has the same sightline over the head of the average-height person in front of him.

As shown in **8.1**, the exception is where the view is blocked by a person in a wheelchair. To compensate, the sightline that others have over the head of a wheelchair user needs to be at the same angle that they have over each others' heads, producing the effect shown in **8.2** when 80 mm is added to the bottom tier rise.

The 80 mm calculation is qualified. It assumes, with reference to relevant anthropometric diagrams in Chapter 3, that the head of an average-height person in a typical standard wheelchair is 70 mm above that of an average-height person in a fixed seat, with 10 mm added to take account of the more forward position of the seat of the wheelchair when measured against a fixed seat. The 70 mm condition is based on the wheelchair having a seat height of 490 mm and a fixed seat a height of 420 mm, and elsewhere the geometry of the matter is problematical. To cater for variations the $y + 80$ mm dimension could be increased to $y + 100$ mm or $y + 120$ mm. The same would apply whatever the configuration of the tiered seating; that the y dimensions in **8.1** happen to be 600 mm and the x dimensions are 900 mm is of no significance.

The six wheelchair spaces at the Arc cinema are all in places where fixed seats can readily be removed. The sightlines they afford and the requirement that people in wheelchairs should not obstruct the view of others is considered with reference to **8.2**. Unlike the Arc cinema where viewers look up and each tier is only some 110 mm higher than the next, **8.2** shows seats from which viewers look down, with each tier being 550 mm higher than the next. But in both cases, as in any other auditorium, the sightline issues with regard to wheelchair users are the same.

In the Arc cinema the floor level of the bottom row where there are four wheelchair spaces is extended into the raked area, the effect of which, in conjunction with the sightlines of viewers behind looking up to the cinema screen, is that sightlines of those behind are not blocked by the head of a wheelchair user.

As shown in both **8.1** and **8.2**, the design problem is less problematical where wheelchair places are at the head of a tier. Even where, as in **8.2** by comparison with **8.1**, the wheelchair place is further back on account of rails or a barrier, the view that the wheelchair user has over the heads of those below is not significantly obstructed.

As shown on the **8.4** plan, the wheelchair spaces in the Arc cinema are 1400 × 800 mm. Both for wheelchair users in the front and back rows there is ample room for a direct approach to be made, the effect being that an 800 mm width is satisfactory. Where, as is not the case at the Arc, a tight turn has to be made when entering or leaving a wheelchair space, the important dimension is from the back of the wheelchair to the wall behind. A factor here is the width of the wheelchair space or spaces, with less room behind being needed where they are as in **8.3a** rather than **8.3b**. In this connection relevant diagrams in Chapter 5 are **5.18–21** and **5.36**.

In **8.3** the wheelchair users are in a standard-size chair with feet at the front edge of the space, and an effect of this is that the wheelchair place next to the fixed seating where a companion is sitting is conveniently placed for conversation and other communications. Where, as in **8.2**, there is a barrier in front of the wheelchair and the user is sitting further back, communications may be hindered.

Account of this was taken in the planning of the Arc cinema seating. In the front row the line of the seats is curved so that wheelchair user and companion can sit adjacent to each other, with space in front of them for others who are passing to reach their seats. In the back row the front-to-front dimension between seats is 1170 mm rather than the 850 mm of other rows, the effect of which is that a person in a wheelchair in one of the wheelchair spaces can place the wheelchair so that they are alongside their companion.

With two seats being removed, the place normally used by a person in a wheelchair who visits the Arc cinema is the one at the end of the back row; this is preferred to spaces at the front of the auditorium, a consideration being easier evacuation in the event of a fire.

The Arc cinema does not have good parking facilities for disabled people and is not at the same level as the building entrance – to reach it there is a lift. The report from the management is that it is visited about once per month by a person in a wheelchair.

Hotel guestrooms

The universal design principle of extending the accommodation parameters of normal provision is applicable to the planning of hotel guestrooms. The rule is that wherever practicable standard rooms for the generality of guests should be designed to be accessible to wheelchair users and other disabled people, with there then being no supplementary requirement for rooms that are differently planned in order to cater for certain groups of disabled people. On this basis, special provision is appropriate only in respect of a proportion of guestrooms where particular fittings and equipment are installed or can be made available, for example to serve deaf people, blind people or wheelchair users.

Guestrooms with regard to Part M

The larger the guestrooms are, the more readily the universal design aim is achievable.

In recent years the guestrooms in new hotels in Britain have customarily been planned to more spacious standards than they were ten or fifteen years ago. In 1987 a typical guestroom was in a shell size 3.6 × 6.0 m, i.e. an area of 21.6 m^2, and it was to these dimensions that an example of an 'accessible' guestroom, meaning one designed to suit wheelchair users, was shown in the 1987 Part M approved document; the same example was shown in the 1992 and 1999 approved documents. Diagram **8.5** shows its plan, drawn to the same scale (1:150 on the printed page) as the other hotel plans in **8.6–8**. The 1500 mm diameter circle in the bedroom area indicates turning space for wheelchair users.

The advice in the 1999 Approved Document is that requirement M2 will be satisfied if one guestroom out of 20 in a hotel is suitable in terms of size, layout and facilities for use by a person who uses a wheelchair. An effect of this when new hotel buildings are planned is that it has become standard practice for hotel companies to have special guestrooms designated for disabled people, ones that are demonstrably different from other guestrooms.

The guestrooms in the three London hotels examined in this chapter are in large buildings which have been recently converted from a former use, and none have been taken from hotel companies' schematic guidance for standard room plans, although in each case RHWL Architects followed the company's style brief. The plans for each of the three show a 'standard' guestroom alongside a special 'for-the-disabled' guestroom. In the analysis which follows, the accessibility to wheelchair users of the standard rooms is considered, and wheelchair users with dotted outlines are shown in them.

The special guestrooms shown in the three hotels have an average area of 33.7 m^2, i.e. 56 per cent more than the Part M example. The standard guestrooms in **8.6–8**, ones that are not designed to suit wheelchair users, have an average area of 30.9 m^2, i.e. 43 per cent more than the Part M 'wheelchair' example. The

inference to be drawn is that it could be reasonable for all standard guestrooms in comparable new hotels in Britain to be planned on universal design principles, i.e. with wheelchair users not being treated differently from others. Of the three hotels examined, **8.6** is a 2-star hotel (the other two being 4-star) and its standard guestroom has an area of 29.0 m^2, 34 per cent more than the Part M example of a special guestroom.

Entrances to guestrooms and wheelchair manoeuvring space

In the three hotels concerned, as is normal in all new multi-storey hotel buildings in Britain, the entrances to all guestrooms can be reached without there being a need to negotiate steps or stairs, and all entrance doors are wide enough for wheelchair users to pass through.

The advice in the 1999 Part M Approved Document is that entrance doors to both standard and disabled hotel guestrooms should have a clear opening width of not less than 750 mm, indicating a 900 mm doorset. For disabled but not for standard rooms the 300 mm nib rule applies, that the leading edge side is unobstructed for at least 300 mm, as shown in **8.5**. This 300 mm rule may, however, be ignored where the door can be opened by an automatic control.

In **8.6–8** the space inside entrance door in all cases is of the order of 1200 mm wide, meaning that 300 mm nibs could be associated with 900 mm doorsets. But as noted earlier and shown in **5.31**, **5.33** and **5.34** on pages 50 and 51, the 300 mm nib is not essential for independent wheelchair users, meaning that standard guestrooms whose entrance doors do not have a 300 mm nib will not therefore become inaccessible to wheelchair users and other disabled people; the proviso, one that is a Part M condition, is that they should have doors with 750 mm clear openings.

In none of the **8.6–8** standard guestrooms would space for manoeuvring a wheelchair in the bedroom area be a problem.

Bathrooms

In the planning of hotel guestrooms with regard to universal design, the key feature is the en-suite bathroom – the way it is designed determines the usability of the guestroom for disabled people, particularly wheelchair users. The issue is considered in relation to each set of the **8.6–8** plan diagrams.

Relevant research findings indicate that of wheelchair users who stay in hotels, some 60 per cent need to take their wheelchair into the bathroom[1]. Of these, most can stand to transfer to use the wc; they are able to stand to transfer in and out of the bath, or to use the shower they can sit on a portable bench seat, one which the hotel may provide. For these wheelchair users it is sufficient to be able to get the wheelchair inside the bathroom and reverse it out, without needing to turn it around. Relatedly, this is sufficient for the chairbound people who can transfer frontally or obliquely to the wc where there is not clear space beside it for a lateral transfer. For chairbound people generally, the bathroom is more convenient if the wheelchair can be turned around within it, there is space to place the wheelchair to the side of the wc, and, less importantly, for the bath to have a platform at its head end as shown in **8.5**, the Part M example.

The 8.6 guestrooms

The disabled guestroom in this 2-star hotel is slightly more spacious than the standard guestroom – 31.0 m² as against 29.0 m². Space in it is indicated for a bed for the disabled person's helper, but an effect of this, along with the lesser overall area, is that equivalence between it and the standard guestroom seems to be compromised, with less space for storage cupboards and other furniture.

The bathroom in the disabled guestroom is larger than that of the standard room – 5.1 m² as against 3.8 m². It has a sliding door and the internal space allows for wheelchair turning and lateral transfer to the wc.

The standard bathroom has an in-opening door, with there not being enough space for a wheelchair user to get inside and close the door. Had the door opened out, this bathroom would have been usable by the majority of hotel-visiting wheelchair users.

The 8.7 guestrooms

In the **8.7** hotel the two bathrooms are virtually the same size; the disabled bathroom is 6.0 m² and the standard bathroom 5.9 m². The disabled bathroom is convenient for wheelchair manoeuvring. With a 1000 mm width sliding door opening off a 1400 mm wide approach space, it is accessible for all wheelchair users. Within the bathroom there is space for a wheelchair user who has entered forward to turn around and exit forward. A platform at the head end of the bath assists transfer to and from the bath. The wash basin inset in a 1300 mm wide desk top is suitable for both wheelchair users and others. By the wc there is space for a lateral, oblique or frontal transfer from a wheelchair. The facility that the disabled bathroom lacks by comparison with the standard bahroom is a shower cubicle.

The standard bathroom is also convenient for wheelchair users generally. Off a 1200 mm wide space, its two-leaf out-opening door gives a clear opening width of 750 mm. Within the bathroom there is ample space for the user of a standard wheelchair to turn around. The basin is the same as in the disabled bathroom. The 800 × 800 mm shower cubicle has a raised floor tray. The space by the wc allows for a wheelchair user to make a frontal or oblique transfer. The bath does not have a platform at the head end but with a bench seat would be suitable for most wheelchair users to sit and use the shower.

This assessment suggests that the **8.7** standard guestroom could without alteration be presented as being convenient for disabled people generally, including the great majority of wheelchair users.

The 8.8 guestrooms

The planning of the guestrooms in the **8.8** hotel was more affected by the structural character and layout of the existing building than was the case with the **8.7** hotel.

The **8.8** disabled guestroom has a bathroom with a wc and also a separate wheelchair-accessible wc compartment. The overall bathroom/wc area is more spacious than the **8.7** example (8.6 m² as against 6.0 m²), but in terms of convenience for its users, whether disabled or able-bodied, it is not so satisfactory.

The disabled bathroom on its own, i.e. without the adjoining wc compartment, would cater satisfactorily for most wheelchair users but it does not give sufficient space for a wheelchair to be turned within it, and the wheelchair user who enters forward will need to exit backward. The supplementary wc compartment, one that is similar to the Part M unisex toilet, has the advantage of a wc that a disabled person can take time to use without inconveniencing the companion who could be sharing the guestroom. Its wash basin is not suitable for washing, grooming, etc., the comparison being with the desktop basin in adjoining bathroom.

The **8.8** standard bathroom is similar in area to the disabled bathroom – 4.7 m² as against 4.8 m². It has an in-opening door but within it there is space for a wheelchair user to enter, close the door behind them, turn around, open the door and exit forward. Its advantages compared with the disabled bathroom are that it has a broad desktop basin and space by the wc for lateral transfer from a wheelchair.

Shower facilities
A standard practice when new hotels are built in Britain is for en-suite bathrooms to guestrooms to have a bath with a shower that can be used by a person standing or sitting in the bath, but not to have a separate shower cubicle as well as a bath. In the standard guestrooms of the three hotels illustrated, one (**8.7**) has a shower cubicle as well as a bath, but in none of the disabled guestrooms is there a separate shower cubicle.

Of the 174 wheelchair users interviewed in the course of the sanitary provision research project, 45 had stayed in a hotel during the previous 12 months, and of these 26 needed to take their wheelchair into the bathroom. In the hotel they had last stayed at, 8 of these 26 said the en-suite bathroom was not very suitable for them, or not at all suitable. For two the reason was that there was not a seat in the shower cubicle provided, but none said the reason was that they could not use the bath but could have used a separate shower had it been available[2].

Where in the guestrooms of a new hotel there are to be shower cubicles, either instead of or as well as a bath, disabled people would be helped were there to be a tip-up seat or bench in them, of the kind shown in **7.82**.

Car parking spaces

In Britain the spaces in public car parks are still commonly planned with a width of 2.4 m. In **8.9** the vehicles are shown neatly parked in the centre of their 2.4 m wide bays; this rarely if ever occurs in practice, and the plan shows that the effect of the narrow in-between spaces can be to deny convenient access to parked vehicles, particularly for pushchair users and disabled people, or egress from them, noting that vehicles are shown without half-open doors. The comparisons are with **8.10**, where bay widths are 2.6 m, and **8.11**, where they are 2.8 m.

In public car parks where spaces are designated for disabled people – the wheelchair users and others who display the badge which entitles them to parking privileges – the advised arrangement in Britain is for bays to be planned with a 3.6 m width, i.e. 2.4 m with a 1.2 m passageway. Relatedly it is becoming common, particularly in supermarket car parks, for parking spaces to be designated for pushchair users.

As **8.13** shows, 3.6 m bays are spacious, giving wide passageways for wheelchair users and others. The occasional exception, as shown on the left of the diagram, is the wheelchair user who accesses a van by a side door which is entered by being pushed up a ramp, or by way of a hydraulic lift which when not in use is folded and stored within the vehicle; the same approach is needed by wheelchair users who have a rooftop hoist for lifting them in and out.

As shown in **8.12**, special parking bays that are 3.3 m wide are generally as convenient for wheelchair users as 3.6 m wide bays.

A large saloon car is shown in **8.14** and **8.15**. The carport shown in **8.14** has a covered area giving space for wheelchair access to the car, with an undercover route from the entrance to the dwelling concerned. The garage shown in **8.15** has an access door at its rear, with there being sufficient space at the side of the car for a double pushchair.

Tiered seating and wheelchair spaces
Commentary page 90

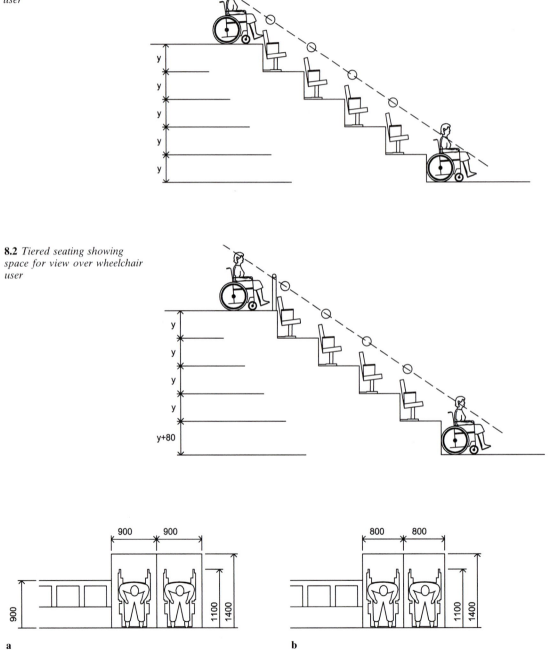

8.1 *Tiered seating showing view obstructed by wheelchair user*

8.2 *Tiered seating showing space for view over wheelchair user*

8.3 *Wheelchair spaces. 8.3a is as advised in Part M Approved Document*

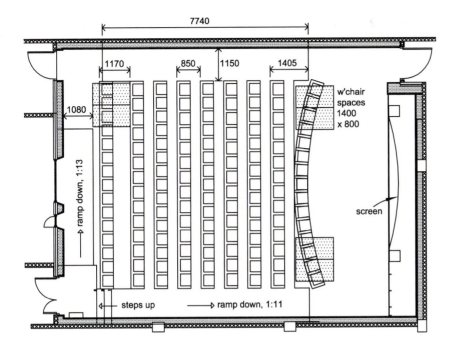

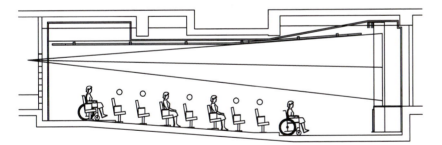

8.4 *Arc cinema, Stockton-on-Tees*

Hotel guestrooms
Commentary page 92

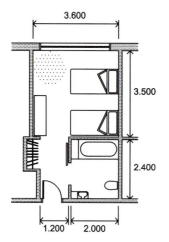

8.5 *Example of accessible hotel guestroom shown in 1999*
Part M Approved Document

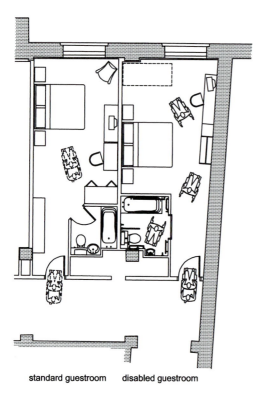

standard guestroom   disabled guestroom

8.6 *Hotel guestrooms in a building in London converted from a former use*

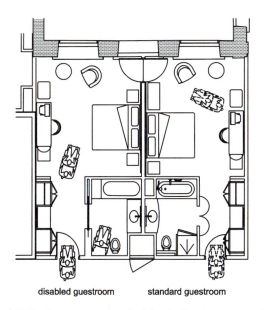

disabled guestroom   standard guestroom

8.7 *Hotel guestrooms in a building in London converted from a former use*

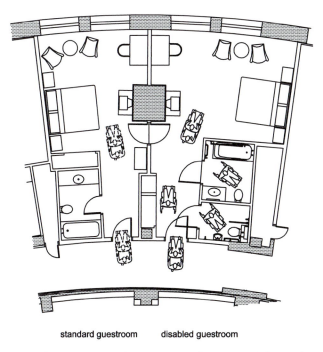

standard guestroom   disabled guestroom

8.8 *Hotel guestrooms in a building in London converted from a former use*

Car parking spaces
Commentary page 94

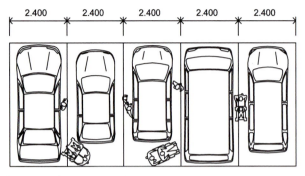

8.9 *Car parking spaces at 2.4 m centres*

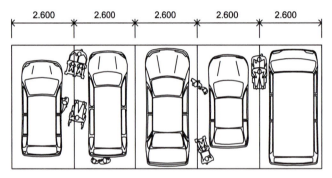

8.10 *Car parking spaces at 2.6 m centres*

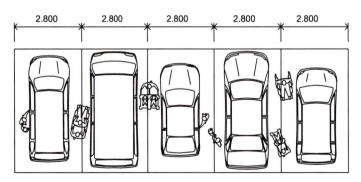

8.11 *Car parking spaces at 2.8 m centres*

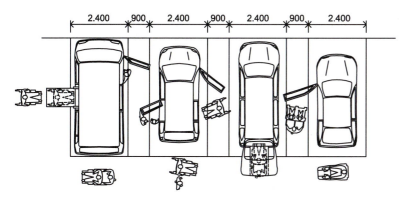

8.12 *Car parking spaces at 3.3 m centres for disabled people*

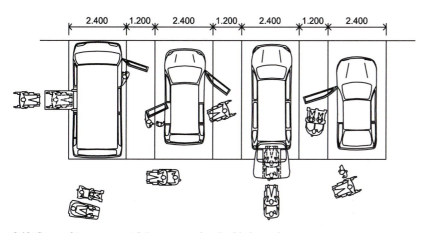

8.13 *Car parking spaces at 3.6 m centres for disabled people*

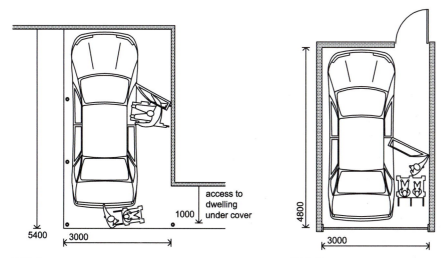

8.14 *Carport*

8.15 *Garage*

9 Housing

The houses designed by PRP Architects whose plans are shown on pages 106–10 are all social housing, commissioned by housing associations with construction costs being funded by social housing grant (SHG).

When looking to apply the principles of universal design, the architects who plan and design low-cost housing of this kind have a more challenging task than when designing more spacious and costly individual houses for private clients. But whether houses are large or small, the aim, as in other universal design arenas, is to expand accommodation parameters.

The standards to which SHG-funded housing has to be designed are set out in the Housing Corporation's *Scheme Development Standards.* No overall space standards are prescribed, but a requirement is that housing environments should be 'accessible'. In this regard the standards for accessibility distinguish between general needs housing and wheelchair housing; the prevailing rule is that when social housing schemes are planned a proportion of them, for example 5 or 10 per cent, should be wheelchair units, for which access to the dwelling and rooms within it should allow for wheelchair circulation and manoeuvre. For the provision of wheelchair units the cost allowances applicable to general needs units are increased.

The plan drawings on pages 106–10 are all to the same scale, 1:200 on the printed page.

Ground floor flats

Five house plans are shown in diagrams **9.1–3**; three are general needs and two are wheelchair units. For wheelchair units a test with regard to wheelchair manoeuvrability and compliance with the Housing Corporation's standard is that rooms should be planned with 1500 mm diameter clear spaces. As is shown by **9.1b** compared with **9.1a**, and **9.3a** with **9.3b**, an effect of this is that the bathrooms in the wheelchair units (both of which have shower spaces) are significantly more spacious. Relatedly, the small bathrooms in the general needs units are cramped and not as convenient for their users. Rooms elsewhere in the wheelchair units are not notably more spacious than those in the general needs units.

The steps in **9.1** and **9.3** are to the entrances to the first floor flats; the ground floor flats have entrances with level access.

Houses to Part M standard

Plan drawings **9.4** and **9.5** show two-storey social housing units that received planning consent before the Part M housing regulation became operative and whose wcs were subsequently redesigned to accord with Part M conditions.

The purpose of the 1999 Part M building regulation as it is applied to new dwellings is that they should be convenient for wheelchair users and other disabled people who come visiting, but not necessarily that they should be suitable for wheelchair users to live in. The consideration here, given that regulatory requirements apply to all new houses, including low-cost social housing units, is that Part M provision should be achievable with little if any increase in overall space standards or construction costs. An effect of this is that the requirement that reasonable provision has to be made in the entrance storey of a dwelling for sanitary conveniences does not mean that an 'accessible' wc compartment has to be in the form of the

Part M unisex toilet for new public buildings. Instead, as the advice in the approved document explains, an 'accessible' wc compartment can be one where a wheelchair user may be able to get half way through the door but cannot get inside and close the door. The associated explanatory plan diagrams are shown in **7.40** and **7.41**, with **7.42–4** illustrating what may occur in practice. Related commentary is on pages 15 and 43.

The accessible wc in the **9.4** house, corresponding with **7.42**, is planned so that it can conveniently be approached by a wheelchair user. The one in the **9.5** house, corresponding with **7.43** and planned in accord with the Part M approved document advice, cannot be approached by a wheelchair user, or only by a person in a small wheelchair who is agile.

For social housing the standard practice is for ground floor flats to have the wc in the bathroom. The three general needs flats shown in **9.1a**, **9.2** and **9.3b** were planned before the Part M housing regulation became operative, with their small bathrooms not being designed to be wheelchair-accessible. The interpretation of the advice in the 1999 Approved Document is, however, that all three would meet the Part M requirement. A wc compartment has to have an out-opening door, but an in-opening door to a bathroom would presumably be admissible if the more important Part M condition was satisfied, that the wc and wash basin should be positioned so that wheelchair access to them is not impeded, and this is the case with the three bathrooms under consideration. Their plans correspond with those shown in **7.70** and **7.72**: if they were placed in general needs units which happened to house a wheelchair user, convenient bathroom usage could be obtained by altering the doors to open out, as shown in **7.71** and **7.73**.

Lifetime Homes
The concept of Lifetime Homes, houses designed to meet the needs of their occupiers throughout their lifetimes, was launched in 1989, and from 1992 was developed and promoted by the Joseph Rowntree Foundation. The design standards for it were initially set out by the Foundation in 1993, and in 1999 were presented with associated design guidance in their publication *Meeting Part M and designing Lifetime Homes*.

The design standards for Lifetime Homes were formulated with a view to their being widely adopted by housing associations for their social housing schemes. They are more demanding than Part M standards, being geared to producing low-cost housing that would be suitable for wheelchair users to live in, not merely to visit. More than any other recent initiative in the realm of the built environment, Lifetime Homes demonstrates the application in practice of the principles of universal design.

The 1999 guidance issued by the Joseph Rowntree Foundation lists 16 standards for Lifetime Homes. Among those that go beyond Part M are:

9. In houses of two or more storeys, there should be space on the entrance level that could be used as a convenient bed-space.
10. There should be a wheelchair-accessible entrance level wc, with drainage provision enabling a shower to be fitted in the future. ...
12. The design should incorporate (a) provision for a future stairlift, and (b) a suitably identified space for a through-floor lift from the ground to the first floor.

Built examples of Lifetime Homes are shown in **9.6–9**. There are no official regulations requiring compliance with Lifetime Homes standards, a relevant item in this connection being the notional through-floor lift, where in a small two-storey house it may be difficult to designate spaces on both ground and first floors that could in practice be suitable when needed.

Space dimensions are not specified in the Joseph Rowntree Foundation 1999 guidance document, but an example of a through-floor lift suitable for Lifetime Homes purposes is shown in **6.24** on page 64. This requires a space 900×1480 mm, indicating that the examples shown in **9.6–9** (drawn to 1:200 scale) are satisfactory in respect of their against-the-wall lift width, but for their length would need more space than the 1200 mm shown on the drawings.

As is customary for terraced and semi-detached social housing, the **9.6** and **9.7** examples of Lifetime Homes have a straight-flight stairway which rises from near the entrance in line with the party walls.

Influenced by a review of Lifetime Homes requirements, PRP Architects planned the **9.8** and **9.9** houses with a straight-flight stairway across the centre of the house, an advantage of which is that there can be wide rooms at both front and back; the comparison here is between the narrower kitchen space as in **9.7** as against **9.8** or **9.9**. The plans assume that if a stairlift were installed it would have a remote-controlled arm which would extend the stair rail at top and bottom in order to provide run-off space for the chair.

The **9.8** house plan shows three bedrooms. Without a dividing partition between the two single bedrooms it would have two bedrooms. Correspondingly with the dividing partition the **9.9** plan would have seven bedrooms rather than six.

In order to achieve high densities, many estate layouts are planned with houses having a 5 m frontage, and in **9.8** and **9.9** minimum Lifetime Homes space standards have been achieved in houses which have a 5 m frontage. In this regard PRP Architects report that housing associations which specialise in provision for disabled people have on occasion requested that Lifetime Homes space standards should be increased; the effect of this where there are three or more bedrooms with a 5 m frontage is planning problems – 5.5 m is more realistic.

Two-storey wheelchair houses

The two-storey houses for wheelchair users shown in **9.10** and **9.11** were planned without there being any particular wheelchair users in mind for them. In both, the location of the lift between floors is shown, but in neither case was a lift incorporated when the houses were constructed; the understanding was that it could be installed should the families living in one or both of the houses have a requirement for it. The plan arrangement for providing a through-floor lift is more satisfactory than in the **9.6–9** Lifetime Homes examples, a benefit being that without a lift there are useful storerooms on the ground and first floor.

In **9.10** and **9.11** the plan of the entrance level wc compartments with space for a shower corresponds with **7.78** on page 88, commentary on which is on page 76. In **9.11** where there is a ground floor bedroom, this provision could be suitable for a disabled member of the household without the installation of a lift, as it could be in **9.10** should the family arrange to place a bed in the living rooms.

The **9.10** and **9.11** houses exemplify the universal design process; they are compliant with Housing Corporation standards for wheelchair units, Part M requirements and Lifetime Homes standards.

Ground floor flats

Commentary page 103

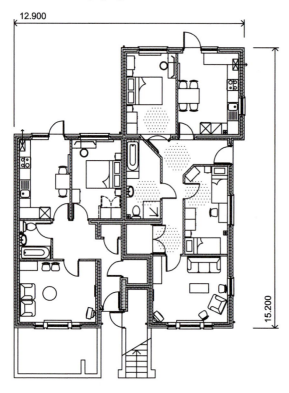

a *1-bedroom 2-person general needs flat, 57 m²* **b** *2-bedroom 4-person wheelchair flat, 80 m²*

9.1 *Flats in two-storey block*

9.2 *1-bedroom 2-person general needs flat, 46 m², in two-storey block*

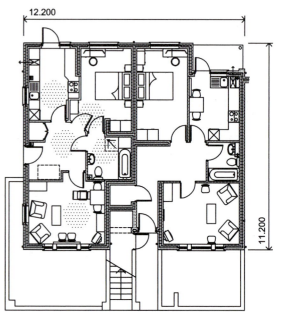

a *1-bedroom 2-person wheelchair flat, 55 m²* **b** *1-bedroom 2-person general needs flat, 47.5 m²*

9.3 *Ground floor flats in semi-detached two-storey block*

Houses to Part M standard

Commentary page 103

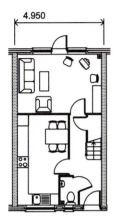

Ground floor   First floor

9.4 *2-bedroom 4-person two-storey terrace house, 76 m²*

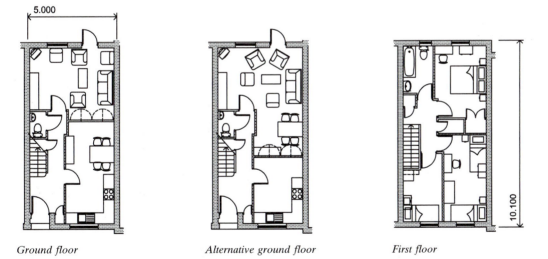

Ground floor   Alternative ground floor   First floor

9.5 *3-bedroom 5-person two-storey terrace house, 89 m². First tenant can choose between the ground floor options*

Lifetime Homes

Commentary page 104

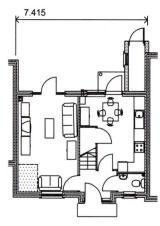

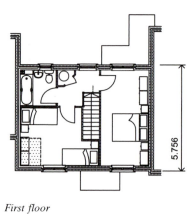

Ground floor

First floor

9.6 *2-bedroom 4-person two-storey terrace house, 78.5 m²*

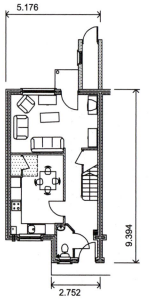

Ground floor

First floor

9.7 *2-bedroom 4-person two-storey semi-detached house, 77 m²*

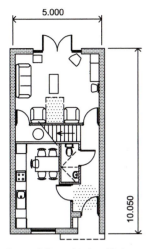

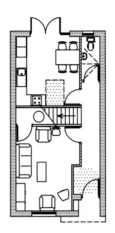

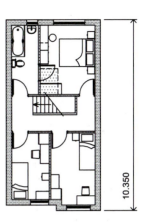

Ground floor, kitchen/dining at front   *Ground floor, kitchen/dining at rear*   *First floor*

9.8 *2/3-bedroom 4-person terrace house, 88 m²*

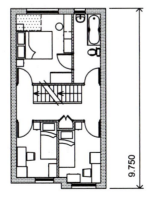

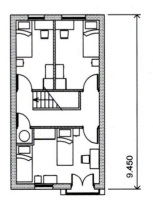

Ground floor   *First floor*   *Second floor*

9.9 *5/6-bedroom 8-person terrace house, 115m²*

Two-storey wheelchair houses

Commentary page 105

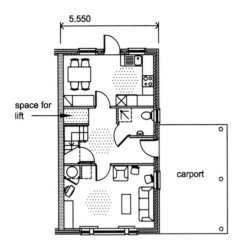

Ground floor

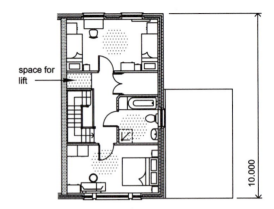

First floor

9.10 *2-bedroom 4-person house, 96m²*

Ground floor

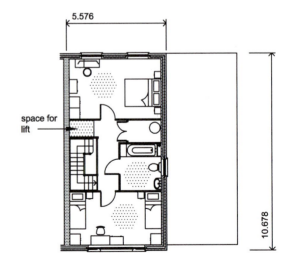

First floor

9.11 *3-bedroom 6-person house, 116m²*

References

Chapter 1
1 Goldsmith, Selwyn (1997). *Designing for the Disabled – The New Paradigm.* Architectural Press, Oxford, p 24.
2 Goldsmith, Selwyn (1997). *Designing for the Disabled – The New Paradigm.* Architectural Press, Oxford, p 179.
3 Goldsmith, Selwyn (1997). *Designing for the Disabled – The New Paradigm.* Architectural Press, Oxford, p 174.

Chapter 4
1 Goldsmith, Selwyn (1997). *Designing for the Disabled – The New Paradigm.* Architectural Press, Oxford, p187.

Chapter 6
1 Templer, John (1992). *The Staircase: Studies of hazards, falls and safer design.* Massachusetts Institute of Technology, Cambridge, USA, p 26.

Chapter 7
1 Department of the Environment (1992). *Sanitary provision for people with special needs.* Volume 2(1), p 153-4. Department of the Environment, London.
2 Department of the Environment (1992). *Sanitary provision for people with special needs.* Volume 2(7), pp 22, 25, 28. Department of the Environment, London.

Chapter 8
1 Department of the Environment (1992). *Sanitary provision for people with special needs.* Volume 2(1), p 174. Department of the Environment, London.
2 Department of the Environment (1992). *Sanitary provision for people with special needs.* Volume 2(1), p178. Department of the Environment, London.

Bibliography

Adler, David (editor) (1999). *Metric Handbook – Planning and Design Data.* Architectural Press, Oxford.

American Standards Association (1961). A117.1-1961 American Standard Specifications for Making Buildings and Facilities Accessible to, and Usable by, the Physically Handicapped. American Standards Association, New York.

Bone, Sylvester (1996). *Buildings for ALL to use.* Construction Industry Research and Information Association, London.

BSI (1967). CP96:1967 Access for the Disabled to Buildings, Part 1 General recommendations. British Standards Institution, Milton Keynes.

BSI (1979). BS5810:1979 Access for the Disabled to Buildings. British Standards Institution, Milton Keynes.

BSI (1994/5). BS6465 Code of Practice for scale of provision, selection and installation of sanitary appliances. Part 1 1994, Part 2 1995. British Standards Institution, Milton Keynes.

BSI (1988). BS5588 Part 8 Fire precautions in the design and construction of buildings, Code of Practice for means of escape for disabled people. British Standards Institution, Milton Keynes.

Carroll, Caitriona, Julie Cowans and David Darton (editors) (1999). *Meeting Part M and designing Lifetime Homes.* Joseph Rowntree Foundation, York.

CCPT (Central Coordinating Committee for the Promotion of Accessibility) (1990). *European Manual for an Accessible Built Environment.* Rijswijk, The Netherlands.

CCPT (Central Coordinating Committee for the Promotion of Accessibility) (1996). *European Concept for Accessibility.* Rijswijk, The Netherlands.

Department for Education and Employment and Disability Rights Commission (2000). *The Disability Discrimination Act 1995: New requirements to make goods, facilities and services more accessible to disabled people from 2004, Consultations on a new Code of Practice, Regulations and Practical Guide.* Department for Education and Employment, London.

Department of the Environment (1992). *Sanitary provision for people with special needs.* Volume 1: Part 1 The practicalities of toilet usage; Part 2 Population needs estimates. Volume 2: Part 3 Tabulated project data. Department of the Environment, London.

Department of the Environment and Welsh Office (1987). The Building Regulations 1985, Part M Approved Document. Access for disabled people. HMSO, London.

Department of the Environment and Welsh Office (1992). The Building Regulations 1991, Part M Approved Document. Access and facilities for disabled people. HMSO, London.

Department of the Environment and Welsh Office (1998). The Building Regulations 1991, Part K Approved Document. Protection from falling, collision and impact. The Stationery Office, London.

Department of the Environment and Welsh Office (1999). The Building Regulations 1991, Part M Approved Document. Access and facilities for disabled people. The Stationery Office, London.

Department of the Environment, Transport and the Regions (1998). Guidance on the use of Tactile Paving Surfaces. Department of the Environment, Transport and the Regions, London.

Football Stadia Advisory Design Council (1992). *Designing for spectators with disabilities.* Football Stadia Advisory Design Council, London.

Goldsmith, Selwyn (1976). *Designing for the Disabled.* Third edition. RIBA Publications, London.

Goldsmith, Selwyn (1997). *Designing for the Disabled – The New Paradigm.* Architectural Press, Oxford.

Holmes-Siedle, James (1996). *Barrier-free Design.* Architectural Press, Oxford.

Housing Corporation (1998). Scheme Development Standards August 1998. Housing Corporation, London

Housing Development Directorate Occasional Paper 2/74 (1974). Mobility housing. Department of the Environment, London.

Housing Development Directorate Occasional Paper 2/75 (1975). Wheelchair housing. Department of the Environment, London.

Martin, Jean, Howard Meltzer and David Elliot (1988). OPCS surveys of disability in Great Britain, Report 1. The prevalence of disability among adults. HMSO, London.

National Housing Federation (1998). *Standards and quality in development – A good practice guide.* National Housing Federation, London.

Pheasant, Stephen (1998). *Bodyspace – Anthropometry, Ergonomics and the Design of Work.* Second edition. Taylor and Francis, London.

Templer, John (1992). *The Staircase: Studies of hazards, falls and safer design.* Massachusetts Institute of Technology, Cambridge, USA.

Templer, John (1992). *The Staircase: studies of hazards, falls and safer design.* Massachusetts Institute of Technology, Cambridge, USA p 26.

Thorpe, Stephen (1997). *Wheelchair Housing Design Guide.* Construction Research Communications, Watford.

Tilley, Alvin R. (Henry Dreyfuss Associates) (1993). *The Measure of Man and Woman – Human Factors in Design.* Whitney Library of Design, New York.

US Department of Justice (1991). *Americans with Disabilities Act: Accessibility Guidelines for Buildings and Facilities.* Federal Register, Washington DC.

Index

Page references in **bold** are to pages showing diagrams